Wild Life

WILD LIFE

Adventures of an Evolutionary Biologist

ROBERT TRIVERS

Biosocial Research
New Brunswick, New Jersey

ISBN 978-1-938972-12-6 (alk. paper)
ISBN 978-1-938972-11-9 (epub)
ISBN 978-1-938972-10-2 (mobi)

First printing November 2015

Book design by Justin Keenan.
Cover design by Steve St. Pierre.

In memory of my teacher
William H. Drury, Jr.

CONTENTS

Studying Life and Living It

For a scientist there is always studying life and living it, and I have never wanted the one to overwhelm the other. Yet that is exactly what a life devoted to science will tempt you into – a life of studying and, otherwise, not much living. Yes, you may have a family and a few good friends, but most scientists embrace a sedentary life, often solitary and intensely internal. You concentrate on experiments and theory and perpetual reading. Your small area of study is the focus of your life, and it is a focus you share with only a few others. Of course, that is not to say you don't have your chances for exciting social interaction. Deep in the bowels of Harvard's Museum of Comparative Zoology, with row after row of specimens along long, dark corridors, occasionally a beetle specialist turns, grabs a gall midge freak, and for one wild moment there is both socio-sexual congress and a melding of lives based on biology itself. He will study beetles, she gall midges, side by side around the world. No competition, only complementation.

But this kind of life never appealed to me. I was an out-breeder, certainly by nature, and I was also raised in a diplomat's home. Foreign countries and languages were part of my upbringing. Since my father served in Europe, I had walked through more cathedrals, museums and art galleries than were healthy for any child, and I had no interest whatsoever in European culture, nor in the academic disciplines based on them. But I did know five foreign languages and enjoyed meeting people in their own land, speaking their language, learning about their area of expertise.

When I finally found my intellectual home in evolutionary biology, it offered me exactly the right kind of foreign travel – in the rural, the bush, the exotic, and the wild. Third world, not first. Evolutionary biology would take me around the world. And it would show me how to carve knowledge from everything I experienced in these travels with a single, very general logic – what would natural selection favor? How would one best survive and reproduce in these conditions? In short, I signed on to a system of thought that allowed me to study life and live it, sometimes very intensively.

I was twenty-two when I learned evolutionary logic, twenty-three when I began studying birds seriously, and twenty-four when I headed on my first trip to the wild. I was single and male. I was eager to see what lay abroad. My biology teacher was an arctic man so that is where I first went. But I did so only once. I knew the moment I left the arctic that I was never coming back – too cold, too harsh, too little life, and, yes, probably too limited a social life. Next time, I knew, I was going south. As it turned out, I was going to Jamaica, where I have now lived for eighteen years of my life.

I have also studied wildlife (and human life) in Haiti, India, Kenya, Tanzania, Panama, Barbados, and Senegal. But it is Jamaica that has, in some sense, been every bit as much my intellectual home as is evolutionary biology. I both joined the island (acquired land) and "stole women off the island," as the Jamaican expression goes. My five children are American/Jamaican. I could easily have gone the West African route, as many evolutionary biologists of the era did. I have often wondered how different my life's trajectory would have been if I had. Certainly, going the Jamaican route did not shield me from exposure to violence.

In evolutionary terms, violence is associated with large, immediate effects on survival. Jamaica, in turn, is a violent society. Of course, I didn't know this when I made the decision to first do my fieldwork there. In fact, I was surprised to meet a German sociologist in 1970 who was studying violence in Jamaica. I thought, wow, a German is willing to travel all this distance to study violence? Must be something interesting going on. He was incredulous. Did I not know that Jamaica was one of the most dangerous societies in the world? News to me. But Jamaica, he assured me, had one of the highest murder rates in the world per capita. It still does.

I think it is fair to say that my decades of fieldwork, especially in Jamaica but also in Panama (and even Amsterdam), have involved more near-death experiences than that of most scientists. I have been involved in robberies at gunpoint and at knifepoint, an armed home invasion, and a fight that led to my being charged with assault. I have also nearly catapulted myself off of heights too great to ensure survival. You might call me unlucky, but I prefer to say that the scimitar of natural selection has often been raised high above my head. In the pages that follow, I have tried to capture this unusual dimension of my experiences where living life and studying it have merged into one another under extreme conditions – precisely those conditions expected to reveal the underlying dynamics of evolution most clearly.

My near-death experiences have made up one very important way in which I have managed not to forgo living life while studying it. But these pages contain much more than just the violent characters and episodes I have met with. I have also met extraordinary minds along the way, from my unheralded teacher Bill Drury, to the legendary evolutionist Ernst Mayr, to the Minister of Defense of the Black Panther Party, Huey P. Newton (both brilliant and dangerous), among numerous others. I have tried to give something here of the flavor of these extraordinary humans, and of what it meant to know them.

And finally I have tried to connect my life to members of *other* animal species, trying to understand them from the inside and even to talk to them in their own languages. In the pages that follow I have woven in, wherever relevant, these distant but often surprisingly familiar viewpoints and communications – that of birds and monkeys, lizards and chimpanzees.

This mixture of recollections might strike some as strange. Near-death experiences. Great human minds. The minds and behaviors of other animals. To me, though, it is the only mixture of recollections that could give a sense of how I have lived life and studied it – and of how these endeavors have so often become indistinguishable from one another. This is my life as an evolutionary biologist – animals, fellow evolutionists, and near-death experiences all in one.

CHAPTER I

From Mathematics
to Viet Nam War Vet
to Unemployed

When I was twelve years old I knew I wanted to be a scientist because it was obvious upon inspection (this was 1955) that none of the other intellectual areas – history, religion, English literature or the social so-called sciences – provided much hope of actual, sustained intellectual advance. I was at first attracted to astronomy, the vastness and beauty of space and the billions of years it had been forming. So much more exciting and awe-inspiring than the seven-day metaphor of the Bible. I got a telescope, read Hoyle's standard Astronomy text and came up with the bi-stellar hypothesis for the origin of the solar system.

I liked that astronomy was a science. These people were not fooling around. They measured things and they did so carefully. They tested assertions against data, and were capable of changing either, and they continually attempted to improve the precision of their measurements. When Einstein's theory that gravity bent light was tested by the apparent change in position of a star during an eclipse we had dramatic evidence, measured with great precision, of exactly how much that bend was. But astronomy was not a discipline you could pursue in the eighth grade, so I soon turned to mathematics.

My father happened to have a large number of math books and out of sheer boredom one day I picked out one entitled "Differential Calculus." I was thirteen and it took me two months to master the book. It then took me two more to master the book next to it, "Integral Calculus." It was a thrill to see that the algebra I knew could generate fields with real predictive and analytic power – it was now trivial to measure the area under a complex curve. That was only part of the beauty of mathematics, and its scientific twin: you could learn the whole thing from the bottom up. That is, if you were willing to put in the time and the effort. Mathematical proofs were entirely explicit, every variable and every transformation exactly described. Scientific experiments, in turn, were described so others could attempt to replicate them exactly to see if duplicate results were achieved.

I mastered other corners of mathematics, mainly number theory, infinite, irrational, limit theory, and so on. I entered Harvard as a sophomore in pure mathematics, but halfway through the year I saw the end of the whole enterprise and it was nowhere I wanted to be – at best, producing work with solid utility but far delayed, perhaps by the year 2250, but of no immediate use. Physics was for me no better, because, for one thing, I had no physical intuition at all. When they raised an object off the ground and told us they had thereby given it "negative energy" I headed for the door. And of chemistry and biology I knew nothing, having never taken a course in either at any level.

So I decided to give up truth for justice and become a lawyer. I would fight the good fights – early '60s civil rights, poverty law, criminal law where you hoped the criminal was not too guilty, and so on. I asked people what you studied if you wished to pursue law and they said there was no such thing as "pre-law" at Harvard, so I best study the history of the United States. I declared that as my major and spent the next years learning about the Federalist papers, the Constitution, Supreme Court Decisions, that kind of thing.

I developed an almost immediate distaste for the subject because it was obvious from the outset that U.S. history, as it was studied then, was not so much an intellectual discipline as an exercise in self-deception. The major question U.S. historians were tackling at that time was: why are we the greatest society ever created and the greatest people ever to stride the face of the earth? The major competing theories were answers to this question. The benefits of having a society designed by upper-class Englishmen was one such theory, as

were the benefits of an ever-receding frontier — that is, the increasing exter-
mination of Amerindians from East Coast to West. The larger field of history
was somewhat more interesting but still consisted of stories from the past,
inevitably biased and lacking critical information — and I saw little hope of
correcting either defect.

In any case, April of 1964, my junior year at Harvard, I suffered a mental
breakdown and was hospitalized for two and a half months. Prior to the
breakdown I went through a five week manic phase, with increasing mental
excitation, decreasing sleep, and near certainty that I was the first person to
understand what Ludwig Wittgenstein was actually saying, even though this
was the first philosophy course I was auditing. I remember very little else
from the manic phase except that I started trying self-hypnosis to put myself
to sleep. It did not work and lack of sleep is what brings on a full breakdown.
Finally one night my friends, who had become increasingly concerned, de-
posited me at the Harvard Infirmary where I could not answer the elementary question, "Who are you?" "A pregnant woman?" "A new-born baby?"
But not, "A thoroughly confused Harvard Junior."

Then came eleven weeks of self-admitted incarceration at three hospitals
for treatment of my psychosis. Incarceration — even when voluntary and in
a hospital — is never fun. You are locked in, no longer permitted to move
about as you like. But thank God by that time the biochemists had come up
with compounds that would knock the psychosis right out of you, and then
hold it down afterwards to give you time to sleep and recover. After my final
release in mid-June I spent the summer reading novels, one a day, and I have
always blessed novelists since that summer. As a scientist, I scarcely read all
the science I was supposed to, never mind a novel, but that summer novels
allowed me to leave my own life and dwell in the lives of others while my
own self relaxed and repaired.

Harvard readmitted me in the fall. I spent most of that semester playing gin
rummy all night long — in other words, still resting my brain. But I also decided to take a course in psychology, since my mental breakdown suggested it
might be a useful subject to know. It soon became apparent that psychology
was not yet a science, but rather a set of competing guesses about what was
important in human development — stimulus-response learning, the Freudian

system, or social psychology. None were integrated with each other, and none could form the basis for an actual science of psychology, so I paid no attention to this subject.

The two law schools I had applied to – alleged to be among the most progressive – turned me down, so I graduated with a degree in a field I had little respect for and no intention of pursuing. I returned home to live with my parents, unemployed, with hopes of finding a job. But first there was the matter of the draft.

I AM A VIET NAM WAR VET

Very few people know – or would guess – that I am a Viet Nam war vet. Yes, I served my country in the United States Army during the Viet Nam War. I was stationed at the U.S. Naval Base in Boston the entire afternoon of my service so I risked no enemy bullets. Since I did not serve abroad I can't become a member of the Veterans of Foreign Wars, but I can join Viet Nam War Veterans associations. I need only write to St Louis where military records are stored to confirm that I served during the war. At times I have thought to do so but never quite got around to it.

My service came about in the following way. In 1965 there was a military draft underway. That is, upon turning eighteen years of age, every boy not going on to college was inducted into the Armed Forces for one day, during which his fitness for further duty was evaluated. If they liked you, you got to spend two years with them. If not, you were discharged the same day with varying degrees of restriction on the chance of being called up again. You had, however, served your country during that one day. If you had gone to college, then the same rule applied as soon as you graduated, unless you were going on for further schooling, for example to become a doctor, a lawyer, or a professor, in which case the draft was further postponed, a bias that led to an over-production in the U.S. of all three professions in the late '60s.

There had been a draft all during the 1950s, and every boy growing up knew there were two ways to avoid the draft, in addition to having flat feet: be crazy or be homosexual, or pretend to be either. I had had a mental breakdown in 1964 and was hospitalized for two and a half months, putative evidence of mental illness. Within two weeks of my graduation from college, my draft letter arrived. You ARE a member of the U.S. Army and you are to appear at the Boston Navel Yard two weeks hence at six in the morning for your formal induction, processing, and evaluation.

Inside the envelope was an enclosure that informed me that I risked up to five years in prison or a $5000 fine (or both) if I failed to tell the government about any of the following. My eyes ran down the list: "Hospitalization for psychosis." My God, I faced five years in prison for *hiding* from the government my get-out-of-the-Viet-Nam-War free card! I was told to have the hospitals that had treated me send letters directly to the government. There were three: Harvard's Stillman Infirmary, McLean Hospital in nearby Belmont, and Massachusetts Mental Health Center in downtown Boston. I called all three and asked that a letter be sent to the government and a copy to me. Only Harvard did both, and its letter said the bare minimum: "This confirms that Robert Trivers was a patient at Stillman Infirmary for two weeks between April 14 and April 28, 1964." No diagnosis, no nothing, but since the context was clear, mental illness was implied. The other hospitals refused to copy me. I asked why. "Because these letters are strictly between doctors." This irked me. I have never liked the circulation of private information that is about me but which, for some reason, can't be shared with me. I doubt anybody does.

THE DAY OF EVALUATION

I showed up at the Naval Yard by six in the morning. There was no Army base near Cambridge, Massachusetts, so the Army occupied part of the Naval Yard to get its work done. We were ordered to strip to our underwear and we were put through our paces, marching – hup, two, three, four – forwards, up-and-down, sharp right, about face, saluting and saying "Yes *sir!*" whenever speaking to a superior, and since we were newly inducted everyone was superior to us. We were then told to dress, given our file, and told to march into the nearest building where we would present our folder to the soldier seated at the first station. After that we had the pleasure of going through some twenty stations in numerical order.

I placed my folder on the table in front of the first soldier. He asked if I had gone to college. "Yes *sir*!" Had they taught me to read in college? "No *sir*, I had already learned to read by then, *sir*!" Did they teach me to read upside down? "No *sir*!" Suddenly, he yelled, "THEN WHY IN HELL ARE YOU GIVING ME THE FOLDER BACKWARDS?" I leaned forward and turned the folder around – and thought, "Welcome to the U.S. Army where we have plenty of time to teach you the right way to do things, the old fashioned way."

While he read around in my file, I was made to fill out a two-page medical questionnaire, which ended by asking if I had any "homosexual tendencies." I knew what they were looking for, but since I believed we *all* had some homosexual tendencies, and since I knew I was already free of any long-term relationship with these people, I left the question blank. I then proceeded to the different stations, hearing, sight, flat feet, and whatnot. Left alone at one station for a few minutes, I took the opportunity to look into my folder (as did a number of soldiers at the various stations) and was surprised to find all three letters from my hospitals in the folder. So much "for the eyes of doctors only" nonsense, but at least I too could now read what those letters said.

As I mentioned, Harvard said the least. It acknowledged in one sentence that I had spent April 14 to 28, 1964, in its Stillman Infirmary. Nothing more. No description, nothing. I loved them for that.

The longest letter was from McLean Hospital, a well-known private hospital outside Boston with a very heavy Freudian bias that specialized in keeping wealthy people in their care for long periods of time. McLean was not a hospital I admired. In those days, insurance for mental illness ran out after six weeks. This was because there was no cure for madness and a good, well-aroused case could last forever, until death did you and your illness part. Freudian analysis required long periods of in-depth therapy four times a week at high prices. Since the Freudian system itself had almost no connection with reality, slow progress was virtually guaranteed.

Let me give an example. My young "work-up doctor" at McLean was meant to produce a Freudian analysis and prognosis of me during my first month there, based on twenty hours of meetings. Throughout those twenty hours, he was utterly silent. He did not answer questions; he did not offer opinions. This was meant to encourage my unconscious to reveal itself to him without any interference on his part. Fine. What did it reveal? One day he finally spoke up and said, "Do you want to know what I think?" Yes! I leaned forward eagerly. "I think you have had an attack of madness." My heart sank. Sweet Jesus, I thought, three days after my breakdown everyone knew I was nuts, myself included. If this was to be my rate of progress I would indeed be in there for two full years or more – as they were telling my parents was necessary and my fellow patients were confirming – and for what? For more pronouncements like this one?

True to form, McLean's letter was deeply pessimistic about my prospects. According to their experts, it was unlikely that I would ever be gainfully employed or function in a socially appropriate manner. At best I would live in a relative's attic, brought downstairs near children only at Christmas and Easter, and then under close supervision. Something like that.

The Massachusetts Mental Health Center, a public hospital whose aim was to give you the right meds and get you safely outside as fast as possible, was considerably more optimistic, though by no means solidly behind me. This was fine with me, since I did not want a glowing report on my mental health record while the Army was deciding whether or not they wanted me. In any case, at lunchtime I went to a payphone and dictated the two letters to my girlfriend so that I would have an actual record.

DID I HAVE HOMOSEXUAL TENDENCIES?

When I reached the psychiatrist's station, I dealt with an officer who questioned me briefly about my hospitalizations and then pointed out that I had failed to state whether I had any homosexual tendencies. Why was this? I said I thought that we all had them. He informed me that you didn't have homosexual tendencies if you had only engaged in a "circle grope." This was, I have heard, what passed for sex among white boys in the middle class '50s – boys sitting in a circle, each masturbating the boy to his left. Nor, he said, did you have homosexual tendencies if you had merely gone down on your best buddy a couple of times. I told him I had not done any of these things yet. You do not have homosexual tendencies he told me, and ticked off the proper box. I thought to myself, wow, this is a very forgiving definition of the matter. I was impressed!

I then went outside his cubicle and waited with my other inductees for the final two men to be questioned by the officer. The second was an attractive young man with a bouffant hair-do, and perhaps a slight fragrance of cologne. We could all hear the conversation. What was the evidence, the officer wished to know, that he had homosexual tendencies? He was a homosexual prostitute. The officer's voice grew slightly hoarse – and where was this? In downtown Boston's Combat Zone. Hoarser still – where exactly? Then a quiet discussion that could not be heard. Long before, "Don't ask, don't tell" there was, "Let's hook up – and the sooner, the better." Or, "Let's have a broad definition of heterosexuality that fully incorporates what we men like to do when we can enjoy meeting in private." The Clintonian solution was the same that Clinton wanted for his own private life – don't ask, and for God's sake, don't tell.

4-F

At the end of the day, I was in for a surprise. I had expected to be classified 1-Y – we don't need you for this war, but we reserve the right to call on you in the future. Instead they classified me as 4-F, unfit for duty in *any* war. I felt insulted. True, one hospital had deemed me hopelessly deformed, but could it really be that, after an eleven-week hospitalization, the U.S. government was unwilling, under any conditions whatsoever, to issue me a rifle in defense of our country? Even if the Russians were coming over the next hill? Apparently so. They did not trust me to shoot in the right direction. I thought to myself, Well, by God, they should *not* trust me to shoot in their chosen direction. I will shoot in a direction of my own choosing, along lines of justice (as I imagined it) not patriotism, and to hell with the consequences. Of course I had no gun and this was all mental posturing, but still why was I being told that under *all* conditions of war in defense of my country I was to be regarded as counter-productive?

To be denoted 4-F in those days was not to receive a compliment. They were known as the "Four Fuck You's" – they fucked you out of employment, therefore social security, and two other things I have forgotten. On the way out (I learned) you were supposed to deliver the fifth fuck-you. You turned your head back to the Naval Base and said, "Well, fuck you, too." And that is exactly what I did. My father was a U.S. diplomat so I had grown up in foreign countries and already had an international bent, but from then on I truly felt international. I owed the U.S. government not a thing, and the same went for them back to me. If you do not trust me to act for group benefit under extreme group danger, then I do not trust you to act in my benefit under any circumstances.

I felt, in the great Amerindian expression, as if I were, "Off the reservation for good," not coming back. I was a free man – of course I was still a U.S. citizen, unlike the Amerindian. But I could think and do and feel whatever I pleased. I neither owed the larger society anything, nor it me. I only needed a job.

CHAPTER 2

Bill Drury,
The Man Who Taught
Me How to Think

I did get a job soon enough upon graduating, and in Cambridge at that. The company itself was a Harvard off-shoot, Education Services Incorporated, set up to attract funding from the National Science Foundation for the purpose of developing new courses for schoolchildren. Just as there would be the "new math" (after Sputnik) so there would be the "new social sciences." I was employed to help with the new social sciences. We would teach five million fifth graders about hunter/gatherers, baboon behavior, the social life of herring gulls, and evolutionary logic, or so we thought.

For the first six weeks my employers had me read around in various subjects and attend meetings. One day they called me in and asked me if I knew anything about humans, by which they meant anthropology, sociology or psychology. I assured them I did not. "Do you know anything about animals?" No indeed. "In that case, you are going to work on animals." This was because they cared less about the animal material. On such minor, chance events, one's entire life may turn. I might have discovered biology later in life, but I doubt it, and I doubt I would then have been in a position to exploit its many benefits.

They assigned me a biologist to guide my reading and sign off on my work. His name was William Drury and at the time he was the research director at the Massachusetts Audubon Society in Lincoln, Massachusetts. For two years, my employer paid him to be my private tutor in biology. It was perhaps the greatest stroke of luck in my life.

Before Bill Drury, I knew no biology. After working with him for two years, I knew its very core. He introduced me to animal behavior and taught me many facts about the social and psychological lives of other creatures. More to the point, he taught me how to interact with them as equals, as fellow living organisms. But he could have taught me all of that and still I could have left his charge without becoming a biologist. The key to my future, which he alone among most people around him could supply, was his understanding that natural selection referred to individual reproductive success, that it applied to every living thing and trait and that thinking along the lines of species advantage and group selection, the then-popular vogue, had little or nothing going for it.

Group selection inverted function while rationalizing bad behavior. For instance, distinguished anthropologists emerged in the late 1960s to argue that warfare and preferential female infanticide had evolved hand-in-hand for the good of the species, to control population numbers. Warfare controlled the number of males, and the killing of female infants controlled the number of females. Thank God this species-centric view was nonsense. Not only did it provide a politically incoherent view of social reality, but even today we barely know what causes species to go extinct or even how to define groups properly. So how could you explain what we do understand (individual life) with what we don't (life at the level of the group)?

If selection worked at that level, I doubt I would have spent much time in biology. But for individual interactions, we have a whole world of facts, from precise measurements of reproductive success under a huge variety of circumstances, to behavioral and non-behavioral observations that are of obvious value to the individual and of obscure function to the group or species. In any case, from then on I was a theoretical biologist. I had wanted to be a scientist since age thirteen. Now, at age twenty-two, I had discovered my sub-discipline, evolutionary biology.

The thrill I felt when I first learned the whole system of evolutionary logic at the individual level, applied to all of life, was similar to the feeling I'd had when I first fell in love with astronomy as a twelve-year-old. Astronomy gave you inorganic creation and evolution over a fifteen-billion-year period of time. Evolutionary biology gave you the comparable story over four billion years. Astronomy spoke of the vastness of time and space, while evolutionary logic did the same thing for *life itself*. Living creatures have been forming over a four-billion-year period of time, with natural selection knitting together adaptive traits all through that time, so that living creatures are expected to be organized functionally in exquisite and ever-counterintuitive forms. As I had when I was first discovering astronomy, I felt a sense of religious awe.

By the way, Bill was a hard teacher. When you were wrong, he was sure to point it out – not cruelly, no over-kill, just the simple truth. If you argued back, he was up to the challenge. That was how I learned what natural selection was and was not. Bill wasn't interested in cradling your self-esteem. He was only interested in teaching you the truth. I liked that. I've always preferred knowledge over-self-esteem. When I brought him population-advantage arguments for the existence of male antlers in caribou, he gently took me through the entire fallacy and then had me read two short pieces on opposite sides of the issue. Three days later I was a complete convert, almost willing to stop people on the subway and yell, "Do you know what is wrong with group selection thinking? *Do you?*"

I was once watching a herring gull through binoculars side by side with Bill. In those days, a herring gull could not scratch itself without one of us asking why natural selection favored that behavior. In any case, I offered as an explanation for the ongoing gull behavior something that was nonfunctional and suggested that the animal was not capable of acting in its own self-interest. Bill said quietly, "Never assume the animal you are studying is as stupid as the one studying it." I remember looking sideways at him and saying to myself "Yes sir! I like this person. I can learn from him."

Another time, we were walking in the woods near his home after I had had a minor breakdown in 1972. It was nothing like the cataclysmic event of 1964, but I'd spent ten days at Harvard's Infirmary. I confided in him that after the first breakdown I had vowed that if I ever saw one coming again I would commit suicide to avoid the extreme pain. But, after this second minor breakdown I'd decided that if the big one came back, I would kill ten people

BILL DRURY. His head was almost completely round – a cephalic index of one – believed to be ideal in cold climates because optimal for heat conservation. (Photo courtesy Mary Drury.)

on a list first before dying in the counter-attack. Was this a step forward in my thinking or a step backwards? We walked in silence in the woods for a few moments before he said, "Can I add three names to your list?" My heart beat warmly – how could you not love a man like this? He could answer your question with a joke that implicated himself in all your basest instincts.

COUNTER–CULTURAL TO THE CORE

Bill was counter-cultural to the core. I have never met an organism who could so often take the reverse view of the common one and still appear to prevail. You think evolution favors what is good for the group or the species or even the ecosystem, the dominant view at the time? Bill thought this was utter nonsense. Why stop there? Why not earth, galaxy, and universe advantage?

You think nuclear war is the greatest challenge to the survival of life on earth? He thought environmental collapse the greater threat. Surely bacteria would survive a nuclear holocaust and regenerate life in other forms afterwards. I agree but I think it just as likely that they will survive ecological collapse, even if it carries with it all living plants and animals. Bacteria have now been regularly found in the earth's crust at a kilometer or more below the seabed. Neither nuclear war nor ecological collapse has any hope of dislodging them.

You think the natural way to argue is from animal to human, the dominant style at the time? He thought this absurd on its face. You can study zebras all your life, and throw all other hoofed animals into the bargain, but what do you then know about zebras or hoofed animals? Next to nothing compared to what you know about yourself. So if you are interested in social theory based on natural selection, isn't it often better to start with yourself and then argue outwards? This is precisely what I then did in my first scientific paper, on reciprocal altruism. It seems obvious from our own lives that friends are often more important to us than relatives, and that the relationship between friends is built on some form of reciprocity – you each do good unto the other – but with a temptation to cheat in your own favor. I started with that observation and stated the argument in as general a form as possible, so that it could apply to any form of life, down to single-celled organisms or bacteria. Other scientists have since applied the principle successfully to both of these, in fact.

Beginning with people is also often the best way to isolate a fallacy. Students used to come to me and argue that females in nature should prefer older males, since they had demonstrated ability for long survival. I would say "no," we are all equally old (about three-plus billion years), we only differ in how far back in time our individual genotypes have survived. Since the whole function of sex is to break up genotypes to produce novel variation that will out-reproduce the prior forms, younger men might be more attractive because they have more recently reshuffled genes. But the clincher was what daily life said. How many times do you hear a woman say of me, "He is ugly, weak and has a nasty disposition, but God is he old. I am so turned on!"

You think monotheism is superior to polytheism? Bill would say, what do you know about polytheism, or for that matter monotheism? You assume monotheism is superior because it presumes to have a single order to the world, a single unifying logic and force, but what does this force represent? Bill taught me that polytheistic religions often had a better attitude toward nature than did the monotheistic ones. In Amerindian religions there were spirits of the forest, of the canopy, of the deep woods, of the gurgling spring, and each captured aspects unique to these ecological zones. For someone like Bill, who had literally lived fifteen to twenty years of his life in the woods, these distinctions were so much closer to his own view than that emerging from monotheism – which basically boiled down to a form of species advantage reasoning.

And consider that in monotheism God is almost always male. According to evolutionary logic, children come first, women (the primary investors) second – last, least, and hardest to justify come males. So why should God be a male? Males appeared late in evolution, and then initially as hermaphrodites, so monotheism gives an erroneous view of God and nature on multiple levels, supporting patrimony, patrilineal name and property inheritance, and many other male-biased behaviors.

On another occasion, Bill and I were discussing racial prejudice and the possible biological components thereof, and he said to me, "Bob, once you've learned to think of a herring gull as an equal, the rest is easy." What a welcome approach to the problem, especially from within biology. Bill was down to the level he taught me to be at. We are all living organisms – make discriminatory comments about others at your own risk. In Bill's view, it was always better to try to see the world from the view of the other creature.

One of Bill's deepest lessons was in how to view other organisms in a way that took into account that the very act of viewing has its own effects. This was the Heisenberg uncertainty principle applied to biology.

The first lesson is to try to see the other creature from its own standpoint, and the next is to avoid affecting its behavior while you watch it. Watching an animal can set up contradictory effects. Many animal behaviorists are unaware of the most elementary facts regarding this interaction. For example, it is true that watching a bird through binoculars brings it much closer to your eyes, but the bird may see the binoculars as a super-stimulus – eyes many times the normal size, hence able to see much further. So the birds fly a hundred meters away from you. What is your net gain? It may not exist.

"Never point" was another rule Bill taught me early on. Through long millennia of interaction with humans, animals might be expected to have evolved cautious behavior toward a finger pointed at them. A pointed finger looks like a weapon or, at the very least, a cue to someone who may have one. Over and over on my property in Jamaica, I have to ask skillful local naturalists not to point with a finger at a bird or a lizard they are trying to show me because the animals are more likely to hide as soon as they see the pointed finger. If they must point, I tell them, at least use a bent finger. I myself do not like being pointed at by anyone else at any distance, so I can well understand how the birds feel. Huey Newton felt the same way – it was always a gun pointed at him, metaphorically at least. If he was your friend, he would duck to the left and to the right to avoid your gunshot, but he was capable of grabbing your finger and bending it away. Bill had already taught me all this via birds.

One afternoon, Bill invited me to go bird watching on his small island off the coast of Maine. I ran for my bird books and binoculars, but he told me to leave them behind. We made our way over to the nearest short tree, growing alone in the open, where he proceeded to make a series of high-pitched sounds. Before long, the tree began to fill up with birds, themselves making a series of calls. The more birds filled the tree, the more birds it seemed to attract, so that soon, as if by magic, all small songbirds in the area were streaking toward us. By this time Bill was down on his knees, bent over and making a deep, moaning sound, his jacket pulled over his head as if he were hiding something.

The birds actually appeared to be waiting in line to hop down to get the closest view of Bill they could. They hopped from branch to branch until they rested on a branch about six feet off the ground and only two feet from my face. Bill would introduce them. "This is a male, black-capped chickadee. I'd guess he's about two to three years old. Can you tell if there's yellow between his back and shoulders [stored fat]? That is a good index of age."

In a matter of minutes Bill had reduced the distance between these birds and us by orders of magnitude, both physically and socially. Our relationship was now so different that I was permitted a personal introduction at a distance of a couple of feet

Later, Bill explained the trick to me. At first, he had only been imitating the mobbing calls of a couple of small songbirds in the area. Such calls are designed to attract crowds of small birds in order to attack a vulnerable predator caught exposed in the open.

But as the birds arrived in the small tree, Bill had begun interspersing the mobbing calls with various owl hoots. The owl is deadly at night but nearly blind and vulnerable in the daytime, and groups of birds will mob it in order to run it out of their area or even harass and kill it on the spot. The prospect of mobbing an owl drew the birds into the tree at an ever-increasing rate, since mobbing assemblages gain in individual safety and group strength with each new arrival. Recently it has been shown that birds are more likely to mob a target if the caller helped mob its own victim.

Once the birds had landed on the tree they could see two humans but no owl, although one of the humans was doing his best to act as if he had an owl hidden under his jacket, from which was issuing very owl-like sounds. This drew them as close as they could get for a good look, which put them two feet from my face. Unlike some tricks, knowing how Bill did his in no way detracted from my enjoyment. Quite the contrary. It revealed the deeper logic by which Bill had permitted me to see and interact with wild creatures at the distances at which they usually interact with each other.

For me, the moment was utterly magical.

TALKING TO BIRDS IN THEIR NATIVE LANGUAGE

From this moment I was hooked. I wanted to talk to birds in their language just as Bill did, and just as I had always wanted to talk to every sub-group of humans in their own language — how else to get to know their own system of thought? The key with birds was simply to mimic them. So I practiced my bird mimicry. In many circumstances, males have a strong tendency to counter-sing — that is, mimic you back. So mutual mimicry could quick-ly generate a social relationship. What exactly that meant to the bird was another matter. Presumably the better the mimicry, the more bird-like the response. One such response is to add variation. As I became better, I noticed that after the fourth or fifth mimetic response by me, the bird would often add a new element, a trill for example, which I in turn would seek to mimic. Female birds in nature, it was later shown, have a strong preference for mating with males who produce more complex songs.

In talking to birds — or other species more generally — the key is melo-dy, and the foundation is Morton's rule: the larger the creature, the deeper the sound; the smaller the creature, the higher the sound. The law comes from physics. The larger the surface area of the drum, the deeper the sound it makes. Which leads to the secondary rule: that deep sounds are associat-ed with assertions of dominance and hostility, high with subordinance and fear. One night in Panama City 1980, two young strong Afro-Panamanians grabbed me from either side while two others displayed eight-inch knives the better to convince me to lie down so that they could extract my wallet. They then walked off, removed the money and threw the billfold aside, an act of kindness I was grateful for. In any case, some Guardia National officers rolled in and asked what had happened. I replied in a falsetto that was two octaves above what I was aiming for. Everyone around me laughed, yet I could not control my own voice. Morton's rule.

I developed a habit of whistling to birds whatever I was saying in everyday English, singing the pitch in the bird's range but having the variation in pitch reflect the variation in my sentence. For example, when I introduced my son to a robin family (in a nest right outside my front door), I would whistle, "This is Jonathan, he is my son." On the letters 'j' and 's' my voice shot up — it is natural to give your son a positive and also diminutive sound.

My son was willing to play more elaborate games where he would stand ten yards from the nest and I would whistle, "Jonny, come here!" (voice goes up on 'j' and 'h') and he would then whistle, "I am coming" (up on 'c') and then run toward me. Whether the birds made anything of this I don't know, but I do know that after several weeks, when I went out back around three p.m. to do my evening show of counter-singing, the surrounding bushes filled up with birds apparently eager for the show. Did they laugh at night among themselves? Who knows?

Can studying animal language this way be associated with my penchant for near-death experiences (see: much of the rest of this book)? You be the judge. Once I was holding my eighteen-month old son in my arms, exploring the nearby trees in our little apartment complex in Cambridge, Mass. Suddenly I saw a squirrel up a tree but no amount of pointing could get my son to see it, too. So I decided to draw the squirrel toward us. I sang a melodious song in what I guessed was roughly the squirrel's sound-range. The song was something about how sad it was to be the lone squirrel with no one in sight, something like that. The squirrel crept toward me, but alas he did so with such stealth that my son saw nothing. I then made my near-fatal mistake. I decided to reverse the relationship: I would suddenly lunge at the squirrel and combine the physical provocation with a verbal threat. The squirrel would take off running. I would have ruined a relationship, but at least shown my son the squirrel.

I was right about one thing: the squirrel took off running, but straight at my throat. In three short bounds he was feet from being able to leap on me and bite, as his snapping, growling sound suggested he would likely do. By then I was ten feet back, halfway up a hill, my hand securely around my son's neck. With one jump and two skilled bites, the squirrel could have killed my child. I crept into the apartment, thoroughly scared – and forever grateful that I didn't have to explain to my wife how an innocent animal conversation had turned into the death of her infant son.

JEALOUS PIGEONS

After I had spent a year or so watching herring gulls and other sea birds with Bill, I wanted to start a project on a species of my own, a species that I could study on land. I believe I suggested the lesser marsh wren, a species whose social behavior and ecology had not yet been studied. Drury immediately batted down that idea. He said it would take me eighteen months to find the species on a regular basis and another eighteen months to acclimate individuals sufficiently to my presence to permit detailed behavioral observations. That it had not yet been studied, he said, might better be taken as a warning than as an invitation.

He suggested I go in the other direction. Study the pigeon, he said. They were everywhere in Cambridge and too common and ugly to attract any ornithologist since Charles Whitman wrote his 1919 monograph. The variability in feather patterns that helped make them ugly also made individuals easy to identify, so behavioral observations of known individuals could begin right away without the need to capture and handle the birds. As it turned out, there were pigeons that roosted on the roof of the house next door to the North Cambridge third-floor apartment where I was living. They could provide a steady stream of behavioral observations right through the night.

What soon became clear in this monogamous species was that males were sexually much more insecure than were females, and males acted to deprive their mates of what they would be perfectly happy to indulge in themselves, that is, an extra-pair copulation. For example, the group outside my window began with four pigeons who made up two mated couples. They slept next to each other in the gutter of the roof of the house next door. They often settled on the roof any time after four in the afternoon. When spending the night together as a foursome, the two males, although they were the more aggressive sex, always sat next to each other with each one's mate on the outside. By sitting next to each other the males could ensure that each one was sitting between his mate and the other male.

Then, for a period of several days, a new male arrived and was regularly attacked by each of the two resident males and driven off. After four or five days of persistence, the new male was still sleeping twenty yards down the gutter from the other four pigeons, and subject to attack without notice. But the very day he arrived with his own mate, the distance to the other birds was cut in half, suggesting that male concern about male visitors might be associated with some sexual threat or increased chance that his mate would indulge in extra-pair copulation. More striking still, when the third couple managed to join the other two, it was no longer possible for each male to sit between his own mate and all other males. What happened then was that the outermost males kept their mates on the outside, thus sitting between their mate and the other two males, but the innermost male forced his female onto the sloping roof in front of them, rather than allow her to sit between him and his neighbor to the right. The female was not happy with this situation and would return to the more comfortable (and warmer) gutter, only to be forced back onto the sloping roof. Sometimes she would wait for him to fall asleep and would slip down beside him unnoticed, but I would soon hear roo-koo-kooing out my bathroom window and would rush to see her pushed back onto the roof.

This, for me, was a surprising observation because it put the lie to the notion, so common in ornithology and evolutionary thinking at the time, that the monogamous relationship was one without internal conflict. Here was a male willing to force his own mate, mother of his offspring-to-be, up onto the sloping roof all night long because of his sexual insecurities. This suggested relatively strong selection pressures.

Whitman (1919) reported a sex difference in behavior upon viewing the partner in adultery that I thought was instructive along these same lines. Whitman said that when a male pigeon saw his female about to begin copulating with another male, he flew straight at the second male, attempting to knock him off her. That is, he interrupted the copulation as soon as possible. By contrast, a female seeing her own mate involved in the same behavior would not attempt to stop the copulation but would intervene immediately afterward, separate the couple, and act aggressively to keep the other female away from her mate. What was going on here? The obvious answer was suggested by the relative investment of the two sexes in the offspring, certainly at the time of copulation. The male's investment at copulation is trivial, or relatively minor, but the female's investment may be associated with a year's worth of reproductive effort. Thus, males chosen as extra-pair partners by females enjoy the possibility of a large immediate benefit (paternity of offspring who will be reared by the female with the help of another male) and similarly inflict a large cost on the "cuckolded," or genetically displaced, male. These large potential selective effects would explain both a male's eagerness to indulge in such extra-pair copulations and his anxiety that his own mate might act similarly!

The rest was easy. After a few months of observation it became clear that the pigeons suffered from the same kinds of psycho-sexual behaviors and feelings we did: male attempts at extra-pair copulations, combined with male concern that their mates would do precisely the same thing. It did not take long to realize that relative parental investment in the offspring – that is, how much the males or females of any particular species invest in raising their offspring – determined whether it would be males competing for female partners (high female parental investment) or the other way around (high male). With that and the later insight of Ernst Mayr, Bill's teacher, I had the entire outline for a theory of the evolution of sex differences. And all because Bill said, "Try pigeons."

MY ONE TRIP TO THE ARCTIC

My first trip to the wilds took place before I had even had a biology course, while I was still writing children's books for a living. Since my first such book had been on the caribou and its antlers, and since Bill had spent part of his life in the arctic, he got me attached to a Canadian Wildlife Service expedition, studying caribou in the Canadian far North. More precisely, the expedition was shooting a hundred caribou every three months, as part of a study of parasite load. Caribou numbers had declined from three million to three hundred thousand in the previous decade. No one knew why, and few wanted the plunge to go all the way to extinction. Wolves were not the problem – their numbers were controlled by their prey, not the other way around. Could it be diseases?

I respected the hunters on the trip and the entomologists associated with them. When a Canadian Wildlife Service hunter shot at a caribou, there was no wounded victim limping offstage. The caribou dropped to the ground, stone dead. Nor was his or her death wasted (from a human standpoint). Immediately, the carcass was hauled back for parasitological inspection. The visual cues were the pupae or late larvae of flies, such as nose-bot flies. It was astonishing to see the entire nasal cavity of a deer nearly completely occluded by a series of fat insects the size of the tip of your thumb. These were waiting to finish molting in July, drop to the ground, and emerge as adult nose-bot

RED AIRPLANE. My plane is about to take off from our frozen lake. The caribou are all females migrating north to breed; note some still have the antlers they carried throughout the winter, evolved possibly to protect excavated patches of tundra from other hungry females. (Photo courtesy Robert Trivers.)

flies, females seeking out males and then the nasal passages of caribou, within which to lay their eggs. In short, the insect had a month-plus long life as an adult on its own, and nearly eleven months as a growing parasite within a caribou. Similar insects could be found underneath the caribou's skin, equally large and abundant, with females again depositing their eggs during a brief adult stage in the summer.

There was one memorable day for me at the main camp. The caribou females streaming toward us − or, rather, toward the calving grounds behind us − began splitting to the right and the left far earlier than usual. Whenever they split, it was because they were apprehending that danger lay ahead, but on this day they also knew that danger lay behind. They were being followed by five wolves, as the Director of the expedition explained to me. I wanted

CARIBOU AND ME. This female had either not bred or lost her calf. She was curious whom or what was crawling toward her and approached to within eight feet, while I froze to take this picture. Nearest ever to a wild stranger, one on one. (Photo courtesy Robert Trivers.)

to see the wolves, but that was not an easy matter. The dogs were mere flecks on the horizon, and I have been near-sighted from youth.

The Director set me up between two Innuit (Eskimo) men, in their 40s or 50s, one on each side of me, and each one held out both hands flat and parallel to the ground, one above the other. They thereby created a very narrow but wide visual space, whose position on and below the horizon they were continuously varying. They tried to get my hands aligned with theirs, constantly raising one and then the other, then lowering both so as to create different flat, horizontal spaces. Suddenly my view was filled with five dots, each next to the other and each one moving. Wolves! A rare sight in the Arctic. But you had to perform an unusual visual trick to see them, and of

FEMALE AND NEWBORN. This youngster was born about twenty minutes earlier. Within the hour it can run as fast as a human, within three as fast as its mother. The result of selection pressure of wolves. (Photo courtesy Robert Trivers.)

course the locals knew the trick.

Although I respected these people, their life was not mine. I wanted to watch animals alive and leave them alive at the end of the interaction. So I asked if I could see the calving grounds, where thousands of females gave birth within a few weeks of each other after traveling hundreds of miles. The synchrony was believed to have evolved in response to predators – the more calves being born per unit time, the greater the chance of overwhelming whatever predators were present.

I was duly shipped off in a four-seat, two prop plane from the main camp to the calving grounds themselves. There was me, all of twenty-four years old, an eighteen-year-old pilot, and an Inuit man of about fifty in back. It was his job to set up my camp so that I could actually survive for two days until they came back for me. The pilot spent the trip flying in giant loops, muttering all the while that he was not getting enough flying time. With full sympathy for my Eskimo friend in back, I wished the pilot would reserve all these unnecessary loops for the return trip. Although it was June, we landed on ice seven feet thick. My companions waited just long enough to set up a nice, secure tent for me and then flew off. They had only been gone five minutes when I realized I had left my sixteen peanut butter sandwiches back at base camp. Fortunately I had just enough beans to see me through. A lifelong habit claiming its cost every week anew — rushing off without something critical to where you are going.

What followed — all-bean diet notwithstanding — were among the most beautiful two days of my life. I was completely cut off from all other human beings. There was no evidence that they were nearby (as indeed they were not), nor that they had ever had been in the area. No planes flew overhead, no artifacts were visible on the partly snow-covered tundra. Nothing. It was just the caribou, me, and the brown bear, the most dangerous predator, though said to be very infrequent. The daytime was long, about eighteen hours, plenty of time to crawl around near the caribou, trying to get as close to the blessed event as possible while keeping enough distance so as not to disturb them.

I came to within a half-hour of several births and also noticed an interesting fact: females like to congregate in small groups within the larger assemblage. You would think it would be easier to crawl up on a lone female with a calf than a female with others nearby. You would be wrong. When the female near others spots a movement from you, she looks straight at you (while you freeze) then she looks around at the other females. Since all of them are grazing, heads down, she does likewise. Not so if she is alone. She stares right at you, looks around and sees that there is nobody nearby and promptly runs toward the nearest female. I was later to learn that this was a major force in forming groups – the "selfish herd effect" – each animal wishing to join others in the face of one or more predators, not the better to spot the predator but, rather, to reduce the per capita chance of being sought out and caught within a larger group. Safety in numbers.

I GET TO KNOW SOME LOCALS

The town where we initially encamped until weather permitted us to fly into the bush was split into an Eskimo section and a "white" one. The two communities came together almost every night to watch movies. I soon noted something of interest. I did not know which of the Eskimo women were good-looking. I unconsciously thought the best-looking were those who were most European in appearance. That is not how the Eskimos saw it. You could easily spot where the hip and popular young Eskimos were seated, and I soon saw the women through Eskimo eyes: long beautiful faces, slanting eyes, no ugly nasal protrusion to destroy the effect.

I was later to learn something similar in Jamaica. When I first went there I learned that "split tooth gal" were especially sexy – that is, women with a gap in the middle of their front incisors. Made no sense, but trust me, within a year or two I was fully aboard – and up to this blessed moment, I am at once attracted to a "split tooth gal." (Split tooth men are also said to be attractive to the opposite sex, but less so.) The local culture teaches you what is locally attractive, if you only pay attention. And, when you do, you are pleasantly surprised at the speed of your adjustment.

By the way, I did manage to chat up two Eskimo women (not the beautiful ones, of course) to the point where they were willing to invite me back to their home. Back we went to a long wooden building, within which were partitions and even hung blankets, but I scarcely comprehended their meaning. The evening wore on, reaching three a.m. with me still trying to figure out how to separate the one I thought I wanted from her friend. (For all I know in retrospect, a threesome might have gone better.) But I was young and naïve and thoroughly surprised when after making a joke I heard a third individual laugh within the large room. It didn't sound like a woman.

I realized then that the situation was more complicated than I had supposed and a spirit of caution seized me. I shortly took my leave, the women kindly pointing out the need for me to walk carefully along the boundaries of the various Eskimo properties. Each had a large, chained dog who could reach the outer edges of the owner's property but not enough to keep you from slipping between boundaries. I remember these dogs were ferocious and later learned that Eskimos often failed to feed them regularly so as to add an extra motivation to their aggressiveness – they would actually eat you, not merely seek to injure you.

BACK TO BILL DRURY

You may be wondering, after hearing for so many pages about this superb artist, naturalist, and bird mimic named Bill Drury, why you have never heard his name before. The truth is, for all his talents, he was not a good logical writer or speaker. He was, in fact, dyslexic. It was up to others to put his extraordinary insights down on paper in a way that would persuade the un-persuaded. I have always considered it one of my greater strokes of good luck that I was given the opportunity to be one of these others.

I do not think I fully appreciated the immense value Bill Drury had been to me until he died in 1992 at age seventy-one. A few months later, one night it hit me and I bawled out, "Where are you now, Bill, when I need you most?" and wept bitter tears – tears for a great and wonderful teacher, warmly remembered, and tears for myself, forced now, at last, to navigate life and biology's waters alone, without a trusted and loving guide who had a deep knowledge not only of animal behavior, but of ecology, botany, geology, and human behavior as well.

CHAPTER 3

Memories of Ernst Mayr

Ernst Mayr was the greatest U.S. evolutionist I ever met, certainly Mr. Animal Species and possessing a very broad and deep knowledge of almost all of biology. He had also perhaps the strongest phenotype of any organism I have ever met. He lived to be a hundred and published more books after age ninety than most scientists do in a lifetime, and not trivial ones either. He was strong in character, personality, and mode of expression. He was also happy to report what others said about him. Whether talking about some arcane point in evolutionary biology, or how correctly to pronounce a word, or the full measure of your own failings, you were never in doubt as to where Mayr stood. I was fortunate to know him over a period of some thirty years, beginning with my own entry into evolutionary biology.

FIRST MEETING

I first met Ernst Mayr in the spring of 1966, in his office at the Museum of Comparative Zoology. I was brought to him by my teacher, William Drury, himself a former student of Mayr's. Under Bill's tutelage I had become convinced in less than nine months that it was possible to become an evolutionary biologist at the advanced age of twenty-three, never before having had a course in biology or chemistry. The visit with Ernst Mayr was meant to reinforce this conviction and to offer me help along the way. Mayr was then Director of the Museum of Comparative Zoology at Harvard, and he operated as Director out of a remarkably small office off his secretary's much larger one. Mayr was a short man, with a clear, piercing gaze, and a warm countenance. After an initial discussion, Ernst told me that it was not at all impossible to become a biologist at my age, and with my lack of background. He cited the case of Richard Estes, who though a journalist in his late thirties and completely untrained in biology, had gone back to school and was now doing a first-rate field study of the social behavior of wildebeest as part of his doctoral work at Cornell. Estes had taken chemistry at night school, Ernst told me, and he urged me to do the same. "Take chemistry at night at Boston University," he said. "Chemistry at Harvard is way too difficult, being geared towards pre-meds and molecular biologists." He urged me especially to avoid Harvard's notorious organic chemistry course. I told him I planned to take a year at Harvard as a special student and make up for my undergraduate education. "Where would you like to do your graduate work?" Ernst asked. I suggested that it would be nice to work with Konrad Lorenz. "No!" Ernst said. "He's too Austrian for you, too authoritarian. Who else?" I suggested that it might be a good idea to work with Niko Tinbergen. "No," Ernst said, less emphatically. "He is only repeating now in the '60s what he already showed in the '50s. Where else?" It was clearly time for some fresh input, so I asked him, "What would you suggest?"

Ernst then flung his arms in a short arc so that they now stood out from his sides and said, "What about Haaarvard?" Dum-kopf, I thought, striking the side of my head with my hand. Harvard indeed! Ernst made it clear that Harvard was very strong in evolutionary biology and that this was the natural field in which one wished to be trained. Although Harvard's only professor of animal behavior had just left for Rockefeller – Donald Griffin, the celebrated student of bat echo-location – Ernst noted that much behavioral work was done within particular taxonomic groups. He had students doing bird behavior. There were behaviorists working on lizards and snakes, and social insects. What Harvard had was the Museum of Comparative Zoology, the Botanical Museums, and the taxonomists to go with these, who served Harvard's interests, of course, by increasing the value of the collections.

I believe Ernst convinced me on the spot. When I arrived in his office, I was thinking as a typical animal behaviorist of the '60s with evolutionary

interests. That is, I was thinking as someone attracted to the work of naturalists such as Lorenz and Tinbergen. But Mayr knew far better than myself that
the larger home for animal behavior was evolutionary biology, and that the
stronger one's mastery of the larger home, the more valuable would be one's
work in one's specialty.

FIRST CLASS

The first class I ever audited in biology couldn't have been better. It was a
graduate course taught in 1966 by Ernst Mayr and George Gaylord Simpson,
the famous vertebrate paleontologist. It consisted of lectures by Mayr and
Simpson for the first half of the course and then discussion of student papers for the second half. Each paper was mimeographed a week ahead of
time and allotted a one-hour discussion in class. George Williams' Adaptation
and Natural Selection (1966) was on the recommended list, and a graduate
student wrote her paper on Hamilton's kinship theory as applied to the hap-
lo-diploid Hymenoptera (1964). In other words, we were up to date.

Simpson, incidentally, was quite a spectacle himself. A short man, but much
softer-looking than Mayr, he wore thick glasses, and his eyes often seemed
to shake, along with his hands. Yet when he stood up to speak, he spoke in
clean, clear paragraphs, no editing required. At times one felt there should be
someone at his side chiseling his words into stone, so well were they chosen.
This is underscored by something that occurred in the class on primate and
human evolution. Simpson began the class and deftly outlined the history of
the primates as revealed by the fossil record, but when he came to the hominid line, he stopped and said that since this was the most interesting part of
the material, Mayr had reserved it for himself. Simpson then sat down and
Mayr got up and outlined hominid evolution. For all I know, he did it better
than Simpson could have, but I know at the time many of us felt bitter disappointment. Anything that Gaylord Simpson had to say on human evolution
would be worth hearing, even if it was wrong. And we had no reason to
suspect it would be.

I remember one memorable discussion involving Mayr and Simpson and sickle cell anemia. After various parts of the evolutionary story had been reviewed – the frequency of the sickling gene in natural populations being associated with the spread of malaria – they had occasion to refer to the molecular mechanism by which the sickling gene worked. I believe it was Simpson who referred to a paper that had just come out in a cellular/molecular journal showing that the change to a sickle-shaped blood cell literally crushed the malarial parasite within the cell. However that may be, there was a glorious feeling coming from that moment and class that evolutionary biologists at their best were the true biologists, those who mastered biology at all its levels, right down to the molecular details when these became interesting.

What made the moment so special was the use of molecular biology, for molecular biologists certainly made no effort to master evolutionary biology. They treated the field with open contempt. When they spoke of "modern biology" they meant modern molecular biology – while evolutionary biology had all the intellectual excitement of a cross between stamp collecting and the study of dead languages.

In other words, molecular biologists were feeling their oats. At their worst, they were insufferably arrogant and ignorant. While they could cow most evolutionists, they could not do so with Ernst Mayr. His area was the entire subject – biology itself – and, when needed, he took it upon himself to master every section and subsection. Put in academic terms, Ernst did not know of outside disciplines only via review papers and books; he read the original articles in the field with care. It did not hurt that he was he was physically and verbally dominant as well.

Best way to put it, *nobody* fucked with Ernst Mayr. That gave us evolutionary graduate students support and backing, the value of which we were only dimly aware. While prominent and even famous molecular biologists could treat distinguished paleontologists or famous systematists with barely disguised contempt, they couldn't get away with that kind of behavior with Ernst Mayr. Perhaps I imbibed some of Ernst's self-confidence because I passed two molecular biologists once on my way into the library and a friend overheard one say to the other, "I have forgotten more biology than Trivers knows." I got a kick out of this because, of course, it said nothing about our relative knowledge now. Perhaps he had forgotten *all* of what he once knew.

TEACHING BATEMAN. I am lecturing at Harvard on Bateman's work in ~1972 showing that with increasing copulation number, male reproductive success increases, while female RS does not. (Photo courtesy Sarah Hrdy.)

THE KEY REFERENCE

For a graduate student, Mayr was the most valuable member of the faculty to talk with. If you had a problem, Ernst would put you onto the key reference quicker than anyone else. Usually he'd be quick also to see the larger context of your concern and deepen your consciousness regarding your own endeavor. For example, when I described to him the Trivers/Willard hypothesis for adjustment of the primary sex ratio toward the sex with the better pay-off, I knew of adjustment of the sex ratio *in utero* in humans, but Ernst told me he wouldn't be surprised if there were adjustment at the time of conception itself, a possibility now confirmed in a variety of organisms.

The most useful reference Mayr ever gave me helped revolutionize our understanding of sexual selection. I was taking a reading course from him on genetics. Ernst did not urge graduate students in evolutionary biology to take the undergraduate course at Harvard in genetics because it was far too heavily molecular and taught no population genetics. Our first meetings dealt with the first several chapters of a book by Whitehead on genetics, but by the fourth meeting I had fallen behind in my reading, and was having a series of thoughts regarding sexual selection growing out of pigeon observations I was making. I devoted a meeting with Ernst to these thoughts.

After listening to me for a while, Ernst said, "Bob, have you ever read Bateman '48 in Heredity?" I indicated that I had not. "Read Bateman '48 in Heredity," he said. "It's got the key to what you're talking about." We then touched on a few more minor points and I departed. I remember not returning for about six weeks and, still not having done any genetics, I dared to try to tell Dr. Mayr some new pigeon stories. Ernst listened for only a few sentences. "Tell me, Bob," he said, leaning into me, "Have you *yet* read Bateman '48 in *Heredity*?" I indicated I had not. He then said something I will always love him for: "Go read Bateman '48 in Heredity. I will not continue this conversation until you have." I left his office with one burning desire: to read Bateman '48 in Heredity.

That evening, bending over the copying machine, my body bathed in its then-green and odious light – testicles pressed firmly to the side of the machine in case the light was mutagenic – I copied Bateman '48 in *Heredity* from the University library, it being free to do so after dark. And that night I read Bateman and, like the Bible says, the scales fell from my eyes. What Bateman had that no one else had was variance in reproductive success (RS) analyzed by sex. This put the whole matter of sexual selection on a more precise and rigorous foundation. Bateman also explained sexual selection – that is, greater variance in RS in male *Drosophila* – by reference to relative parental investment, a concept that had also been used by Ronald Fisher and

George Williams. But neither Fisher nor Williams had analyzed *variance* in reproductive success.

Curiously, I don't remember what I said to Ernst when I saw him again, but I will never forget the profound effect that Bateman's '48 paper had on me that evening, and how it was Ernst Mayr alone who seemed to be aware of the paper (including, in a certain sense, Bateman himself), and that it was Ernst who made sure I read it. It was a mark of his superior memory that he would remember a recent instruction to you better than you would remember it. In fact, as he once told me, he was born with a photographic memory but hid it for many years because of the obvious advantage it gave him in a German education system built entirely on rote memory. He also told me that at about age fifty-five the gift gave way, but it left you with what was still a very good memory.

I think Ernst might have written something like the paper I ended up writing, except for a curious circumstance. When I came to ask him for help with the specifics of my chapter, he pulled out a folder that he himself kept on sexual selection and apologized for how few were the enclosed articles. He explained that he no longer allowed students to remove folders from his office because of a bad experience he had had with his folder on sexual selection. He, like Darwin, liked to keep folders going on subjects of interest, often for decades, so that when he finally sat down to write on the subject he had a rich set of papers on which to draw. A graduate student had seen his thick folder on this subject, had asked to borrow it for a couple of days, and had never returned. And Ernst, his memory for once failing him, couldn't remember who it was. The folder had been thick with thirty years of papers, and its theft had left Ernst without the energy or will to tackle the problem anew.

I once wrote Bateman years later. I sent him a children's book I had written on his work, and asked him how he'd come to do his '48 paper. He replied that at the time it was routine to run choice experiments the wrong way around; that is, a male was given the choice of two females. This rarely turned up striking examples of discrimination. He, by contrast, felt that this was a poor way to run an experiment on mate choice and, without particularly being aware of why, felt *naturally* that it would be females who would

ERNST MAYR AND SARAH HRDY. It looks as if Sarah has temporarily seized the conversation from Ernst, not that he seems to be objecting. He was perhaps more competitive with men. (Photo courtesy Dan Hrdy.)

be the discriminating sex. So he was the first to run experiments in which females were given the ability to choose between several males.

His experiments showed that when females were permitted this choice and males competed for access to females, male reproductive success varied more highly than did female: more males with high RS and more with zero. In science we tend to think of the written record as freeing us from many of the constraints of oral history, and yet here was a case in which an entire discipline, with the exception of one man, had overlooked a key paper, and contact with this man permitted me to be the first to develop a general theory for the evolution of sex differences.

HE WAS A LOVING MAN

Ernst was a very loving man, especially where women were concerned. I will give you two examples, one involving his wife and one involving my own.

Ernst and Gretel had, so far as an outsider could tell, a very loving relationship. They kept a beautiful home in Cambridge and a hundred-acre old-style New England farm in New Hampshire, and part of the pleasure in visiting them at home was a sense of the love that bound them together.

One example of their relationship that amused me concerned a rare case where Ernst slipped up. I was at their home in Cambridge late one afternoon when I asked Ernst (who was describing for me some of the large foreign literature he was handling for his book on the history of biology) who it was who had translated a particular piece for him. He said, "I did." Almost immediately, Gretel interrupted with perhaps a little bit of bite to her voice. "Ernst it was I who did it! *I* translated that paper." Ernst looked very sheepish and agreed with her. Gretel turned to me and said, "Bob, you know that Ernst and I are like one, but *still* it was I who translated that paper." As if in penance, the two or three times Ernst had occasion to refer to the paper in the future, including once that afternoon, he always added, "Which my wife so kindly translated for me."

In the case of his kindness to my wife, we were invited to their farm and arrived a bit late, my very pregnant wife and myself. Ernst had arranged a little nature walk for us through his property. I noticed that he was leading us on a path that led near stream and dale and yet was somehow brushed clean of any underlying twigs and willow leaves. I asked him about this and he admitted that he had been out on his hands and knees since six in the morning, brushing the whole area clean lest my pregnant wife slip and fall. How could you not love a man like that? Of course, he was angry that I'd been late.

ERNST AS A MORAL COMPASS

One value that Ernst Mayr played in my life was as a moral compass. There are very few people who can act as moral reference points in our own lives in any reliable or long-lasting way. Such individuals, it hardly needs be stressed, play a unique role in our lives. Others will argue with us about the morality of our behavior, but their own system will be sufficiently flawed as to permit too many opportunities for us to wriggle out of their indictment. Not so with Ernst. If he had you as wrong, you were almost certainly dead wrong, nor would he change his opinion in the face of anything except strong countervailing evidence.

Ernst acted as a moral compass in many different ways: regarding financial principles, personal vices such as drug use, level of "academic productivity," in family matters, and more. His strongest criticism of me was my continued use of marijuana after he had urged me to give it up in 1977. He compared it then to his giving up cigarettes in his early thirties. He used to smoke two packs a day, he said. When he quit, he did so completely, and never touched a cigarette again because he knew he was too weak: if he took one, he would be hooked again. He looked me straight in the eye when he told me this. I quit for exactly three days. Many times in the '80s it was painful to visit Ernst because of his palpable disappointment in me. I had not quit, and I was not productive. I have never urged someone to smoke in order to become more productive − or a more original thinker. Quite the contrary, I have only wished I were stronger and had been able to give up the habit.

Just before I left Harvard in 1978, a mutual friend suffered a heart attack, undoubtedly aggravated by his own two addictions, to alcohol and tobacco. Several of us conjured up the notion that our friend would only listen to Ernst Mayr, if anyone, and I was delegated to ask Ernst if he would talk with this friend. Ernst listened to my recital of the man's failings in full agreement but was somewhat reluctant to talk to him, since, as he saw it, it would do no good. Some people disagree with advice at the outset, Ernst said, but our friend was the kind who would agree with the advice but continue acting contrary to it. I laughed, enjoying a burst of moral superiority over this friend, when Ernst woke me from my reverie. He leaned forward and declared, "And you, Bob, are the same way."

In 1982 I visited Harvard and told Ernst that I was working on a theory of self-deception. "How appropriate" he said. When I told Huey Newton about Mayr's response, he laughed and said, "But what else would you expect? A person low in self-deception would neither show much interest nor knowledge." So there is perhaps an irony here, that one's guide to an introduction to the science self-deception (myself in *The Folly of Fools*, 2011) may be high in self-deception. But the whole point of establishing a science is that it is supposed to be self-correcting and not based on reputation, hierarchy, ignorance, naivete, or self-deceptive bias. Whatever weaknesses I bring should easily be corrected.

On minor matters Mayr could change my behavior for life with just one interaction. I remember sitting in Mayr's office and talking about "dissecting" an animal, but pronouncing it "die-sect." Suddenly, without warning, his fist came down hard on his desk. "Dissect," he said. "It's dissect, two 's's'. Not die-sect, one 's'. You bi-sect an angle. You dissect an animal." This is some kind of hell, I thought. Here's a man with a heavy German accent lecturing me on how to pronounce English, but the incident had such a strong effect on me that up to this day, while I can abide to listen to many mispronunciations, I cannot stand to hear the word dissect as it is almost always rendered among biologists, as "die-sect." I still correct people at once, much as Ernst did me. A little Dawkinsian meme had been launched in my life and has never decayed, because it was true and strongly imprinted on me. But I do believe its attempt at self-replication beyond me has been an abject failure.

ERNST APPEARS TO ME IN A DREAM

In the summer of 1974 I was working night and day to complete a draft of my paper with Hope Hare on the evolution of the social insects. The data we had gathered and analyzed revealed a striking pattern regarding the mother-daughter relationship in ants. Both parties – mothers and daughters – were expected to disagree over two variables: the relative amount of work invested in producing reproductive males compared to reproductive females (the ratio of investment), and the proportion of males resulting from worker-laid eggs as opposed to queen-laid eggs. Measures of both of these parameters suggested that the mother (the queen) won out in conflict over male production – most or all males resulted from eggs laid by her. By contrast, the daughters (workers) appeared to determine the ratio of investment in their own favor. Why should this be so? Why should the queen dominate one variable while her daughters dominated the second? I was highly motivated to solve this puzzle because, if I could, it would round out the paper I was writing and give it an appearance of "completeness" that it would otherwise lack.

One evening I worked late into the night on this problem without making any headway. When I finally retired for the night, I fell off into a restless and troubled sleep. Soon enough, Ernst Mayr appeared to me in a dream. Both of us were inside an ant nest underground, reduced to the size of the ants. As worker ants trundled by, we could see in the background a large physogastric queen spewing out eggs. Ernst kept pointing at the queen and saying to me, "Bob, it's the chance of the queen dying; it's the chance of the queen dying — that's the key, the chance of the queen dying." I awoke around six in the morning and like a character out of a B-grade movie — in a cold sweat, mumbling to myself, "It's the chance of the queen dying, the chance of the queen dying." I had never known Ernst Mayr to be mistaken in real life, and had no reason to expect him to be mistaken in my dream, so I immediately set about trying to figure out how "the chance of the queen dying" might explain the puzzle I had uncovered.

For several weeks I tried different ways in which the chance of the queen dying might solve my puzzle. Finally, I saw what Ernst Mayr had in mind. The chance of the queen dying was indeed the key variable, for if in a conflict with her daughters the queen were to die, in most species the colony itself would succumb quickly, for only the queen is capable of producing sterile daughters — workers to keep the colony alive. In addition, even if a replacement were found that kept the colony alive, workers would no longer be able to raise full sisters to which they are uniquely related by three-quarters. Thus the queen's death threatened to destroy the colony itself and, in any case, remove the one individual capable of producing highly related sisters. One would expect workers to be very hesitant about inflicting damage on their mother and instead, inclined to give way in any dispute. The queen should then be able to use her dominance to enforce her own production of the colony's males. By contrast, the ratio of investment in the sexes, being the product of thousands of independent acts of care by the workers, cannot be enforced by the queen.

Once, at the University of Connecticut at Storrs, a man in his 60s came up to me after my talk and thanked me for telling my Ernst Mayr-dream story. He had a story in exchange, he said. In the '50s Mayr had visited his school and given a talk. At that time, there was a member of the department, then in his sixties, who always insisted on asking the first question, which was invariably poorly posed, rambling, and nearly or completely meaningless. As Mayr's talk drew to a close, he and other members of the department cringed. To have this colleague embarrass them in front of other visitors was bad enough, but in front of Ernst Mayr, the greatest living evolutionary biologist in the U.S.?

True to form, when Ernst asked if there were any questions, the man leapt in with a long disjointed question whose content, if any, was obscure. There was a pause, and Ernst looked out over the audience and said, "Are there any *pertinent* questions?" From that moment on, my informant said, he was a fan of Ernst Mayr. Ernst had put down their old nemesis cleanly, publicly, and without any implication that this man might be typical of his department. How much better this honest, straight approach than the usual attempt to invest a meaningless question with meaning, fueled by a secret fear that the man may indeed be typical of the audience.

"I HAVE TO DIE OF SOMETHING"

In his later years, Ernst lived in an "assisted living" facility, but since Ernst stayed healthy and strong, the assistance was minimal. He had his one-bedroom apartment, packed with books on shelves and in piles. He ate in a restaurant on the premises, and the only physical change I noticed was a tendency to walk on the balls of his feet, leaning forward slightly. I noticed a number of different liquors in his bar and commented on it. He was not a teetotaler and had often had a drink or two on social occasions, at his home and elsewhere, ever since I had known him. But why so much variety? Ernst told me somewhat sheepishly that he had a number of women who visited him – women in their seventies – and so he had what each one wanted. He also said they wanted more from him than alcohol, but that he did not indulge, "Because I know *neither* of us would enjoy it."

Ernst died at age one hundred. Strong and lucid to the end. Lynn Margulis, a student and close friend, is reported to have said, "Oh Ernst, you have cancer," to which he replied, "Well, I have to die of something."

CHAPTER 4

I Become a Lizard Man in Jamaica

In the spring of 1968, I was admitted to Harvard as a graduate student in biology, and given a small stipend ($800) to do whatever research I wished to do during the summer. At first, I was disposed to fly to Panama. The Smithsonian maintains a research station on Barro Colorado Island, which was itself created when an artificial lake was formed as a part of the construction of the Panama Canal. I intended to watch Howler Monkeys, but my advisor, Dr. Ernest Williams, was going on a collecting trip to Jamaica and he didn't drive. Rather than hire a Jamaican driver, it would be easier, and presumably more fun, to have me as a driver and companion. He suggested that I look at the lizards with him.

As curator of Herpetology at Harvard, Ernest was in charge of maintaining and improving the collections of preserved reptiles and amphibians. He was especially pleased with his collection of *Anolis* lizards, a genus of iguanid lizards whose 200+ species are spread throughout the West Indies, Central and South America, and the southern U.S. The American "Chameleon," found in several Southern states and in numerous pet stores, is *Anolis carolinensis*. These species, especially those spread throughout the West Indies, represent a whole series of evolutionary experiments run in parallel. Underlying variables such as size of island, perch height, body size, feeding ecology, and how many other *Anolis* species were near, gave detailed description of the lizards' niches, so these too could be compared across islands. An additional virtue of these lizards is that they are tree climbing and, thus, in a setting like Jamaica, much easier to spot and capture than are ground-dwelling lizards.

Ernest used every argument in his arsenal to convince me to come with him to Jamaica. He claimed that any fool could study a monkey (that I was sure of) but that it took a real biologist to study lizards (perhaps). He pointed out that if I were obsessed with monkey behavior there was a *fossil* monkey on Jamaica, as indeed there was. Eventually he wore me down and I decided to accompany him. I have not regretted it yet.

As I later learned, watching Howler monkeys would have been at distances of twenty meters or more, with sightings occasional and made from underneath as a group moved between trees. Your great hope on a Howler expedition is for a good view of testicles, so as to be able to determine unambiguously the sex of at least one individual. Lizard work, by contrast, could easily expose you to twenty members of one species per day, within a defined study area, and the identity of each lizard can be established relatively quickly through capture, marking, and release. In addition, as I was later to appreciate, lizard work offered access to the entire country and culture, not a study in some isolated nature preserve. The fact that Jamaicans feared and detested lizards was also an advantage. Known far and wide as "the lizard man," I had power by virtue of that fact alone.

THE HIGHLY CRYPTIC *ANOLIS VALENCIENNI*

In any case, Ernest Williams and I now set out together for a week of lizard work in Jamaica. We arrived in Kingston in the evening and drove in a blinding rainstorm to the Maryfield Guest House, a decaying English great house set on three acres. The beautiful old trees and well-tended garden attracted a big population of lizards. We began our fieldwork over breakfast on the veranda watching the common lizard *Anolis lineatopus*. The males and females warmed themselves in the sun and then engaged in display and aggressive encounters as they reoccupied their territories. These bright, active, little lizards reminded one almost of puppies or kids, enjoying a little social play in the early morning hours.

Ernest soon drew my attention to a more sinister species, which seemed to hide in the background. This was *Anolis valencienni*, which moved in a very distinctive fashion, slowly and in a serpentine pattern. Individuals of this species seemed unusually abundant at the Guest House, and since an *Anolis* of this type had not been studied, I soon concentrated on figuring out its social system. The lizard turned out to be unusual in a number of regards, completely non-territorial, with small dewlaps on females, traits unknown from other *Anolis*. The lizard was also unusual in that it caught insects that were active at night but immobile in the daytime, and hence highly cryptic. Finding and catching these insects required continual movement by the lizard. This in turn selected for extreme camouflage in the lizards. You could be watching a lizard on a tree through very high-power binoculars, be distracted for some reason, and look back without being able to spot the lizard again, even though it had not moved at all.

After Ernest went back to the States, I remained in Jamaica for ten more days, rental car paid out of Ernest's money, hotel, gas et al out of my Harvard stipend. I studied *Anolis valencienni* in the daytime and the city of Kingston at night. Liking the whole scene, I decided to return to Jamaica the following summer for a full three months study of *valencienni* by day and Kingston by night. My standard joke was that upon arrival I took one look at the women, a second at the island, and decided if I had to molest lizards to pay for frequent trips to Jamaica I would humble myself and become a "lizard man." And that is exactly what I did.

Since *valencienni* was highly cryptic and rarely came down to the ground, and I do not climb trees – in fact, am so afraid of heights I rarely advance beyond the second rung on a ladder – I was seeing and catching very few of these lizards upon my return to the island. Although, grounded as I was, I did have some memorable sightings. I once saw a female hanging upside down under a large branch when she spotted an insect on a nearby bromeliad. Temporarily forgetting the separation between the plants (or so it seemed), she darted forth in her eagerness to grasp the perching insect and promptly fell twenty feet to the ground. There was no movement for several moments and I thought I had actually seen natural selection in action. In this case, selecting against being forgetful when you are high up, which happens to be a

ANOLIS VALENCIENNI. Note how extraordinarily cryptic this animal is even when viewed from its side. (Photo courtesy Michelle Johnson.)

lifelong affliction of my own, and the source of my extreme fear of heights as discussed later. I walked toward the scene of the carnage, only to have a perfectly healthy female run off. She had not been damaged in the slightest. Millions of years of natural selection had already acted on this situation, and she hardly weighed a thing.

I BECOME A GREEN LIZARD FREAK

One Sunday, a woman friend took me on a fairly typical whirlwind visit to the countryside. We left Kingston at five-thirty in the morning, drove three hours non-stop to a country home, ate a bloated breakfast, then slept and started in on some serious drinking. Three or four hours later, we headed back to Kingston. But not before, in this case, the fourteen-year-old brother of my friend climbed a tree in order to bring down a giant, green lizard from the upper reaches of a mango tree. He had seen my excitement when I was shown the lizard and asked if I would like to hold it. Of course I would. That was how I discovered my way around this nonsense of a man who couldn't climb trees studying tree-climbing species. Jamaica had no shortage of youngsters in their early teens who were no longer attending school and only too eager to climb trees and catch lizards for good pay.

Over the next few weeks I returned to Southfield several times to hire these teenage boys to catch lizards for me. The lizard my friend's brother had fetched for me had been a giant Anole. There are numerous such giant Anoles in the world (five species on Cuba alone) but no one had ever studied one, and I was immediately attracted to doing so. Since I now had ready access to them through my young helpers, I decided to make a full study of the green lizard. It was a capture/recapture study that required – fortuitously enough – that I visit Jamaica every three or four months in order to determine survival and growth rates, and, later, rates of reproduction as well. In order to recognize the lizards upon recapture, we cut off their toenails in unique patterns since toenails do not grow back. We also painted a number on each lizard's back for identification without recapture, but since lizards shed their skin every month, they needed to be regularly recaptured for repainting.

This was the start of my first long-term study. What began with a fourteen-year-old boy climbing a tree while I was on a one-day excursion, was to last for three years and become part of my doctoral thesis at Harvard. I returned to Jamaica regularly over those three years and, when in the countryside, I stayed in the home of a woman for whom I gained enormous respect, Miss Nini. She was old enough to be my mother, and later became my mother-in-law, so I was very respectful in her yard – indeed in her larger community. But I still drove every weekend to Kingston.

LIZARDS AS OBJECTS OF TERROR

Most Jamaicans – man and woman alike – detest lizards roughly the way Americans detest rats. Almost every Jamaican woman I know has a horror story of a close encounter of the lizard kind. Often the stories go like this: a croaking lizard falls from the ceiling at night, landing on the woman in bed; she begins screaming and tearing off her nightclothes, eventually running naked from the house so as to escape the odious feel of the lizard on her skin. Or, she reaches for a broom and, instead of wood, her hand curls around the flesh of a wonderfully camouflaged coffee lizard. These women still recall the awful moment when their hands touched lizard flesh instead of wood.

Most men are no more comfortable with lizards than are women. Nothing cuts short an interaction with police – at a roadblock, for example – quite as quickly as my answer to their question, "And what are you doing on this island?" "Well," I say, often moving slightly toward them, "I study *lizard* malaria in Black River!" There is invariably a short pause, followed by "Alright then, gwaan about your business!" They are only too happy to be rid of me. Only once was there an exception. An officer at the roadblock asked if I could test for AIDS. For one wild moment I was tempted to say, "Yes." How else would I ever have the chance to stab a police officer in the back of his hand with a knife (to draw his blood, that is) and get away with it? But my better judgment kicked in, and I declined.

My close relationship with such a hated creature as the lizard has led to some very interesting interactions. When locals first saw large green lizards

MALE IN TREE. A male such as was first caught for me in the wilds of rural Jamaica. (Photo courtesy Robert Trivers.)

emerging from the canopy with numbers written on their backs in white, they believed someone was trying to use some heavy Obeah on them. Obeah is the Jamaican equivalent of Haitian Voodoo: religion, medicine, and psychological warfare all rolled into one. When they learned it was me doing the painting, they believed I was trying to frighten them toward some end, using numbers on lizards to mess with their brains. In fact, lizards do have special significance in Obeah, a point driven home to me by a visit to the vast Carnation Market in Kingston, where you can find for sale everything that's ever been grown on the island. One day I went to the "wood" section, where you can get roots and unusual country plants, in order to fill a prescription written for me by the famous balm-yard healer, Mother Rita, as an antidote to excessive ganja (marijuana) consumption. (She also suggested I consume a lot of watermelon.) When the men asked me what work I did, I said I was a "scientist" – not knowing that this is a term for an Obeah man. They looked surprised and excited. And what was my specialty? "Lizards." They jumped back. "Whaaa, a lizard scientist you be!"

My unusual affinity has also come in handy on more than one occasion. Once, the famous and dreaded "Bag and Pan," a Black River police officer notorious for harassing the poor and helpless, showed up in my study site off a dirt road in his jeep and told my lizard workers to summon me. As I walked toward him with four common lizards stuck between my fingers, I saw that he had drawn his gun and placed it between his legs – presumably as an act of intimidation. But in this situation his move struck me as comical. I knew that if I were suddenly to lean forward, look him straight in the eye, and pitch my lizards right on him while reaching for his gun, I would reverse our relationship exactly, he now with my lizards, me with his gun. As it was, he asked what I was doing and, hearing that it involved lizards, was soon on his way.

The Jamaican fear of lizards can also come in handy in less threatening contexts. The Jamaican banking system is notoriously slow in making your money available to you and, having once waited nine days in vain for money wired from the States that had reached Kingston but not yet my Black River account, I was compelled to inform a bank employee that I intended to return in two hours with three large green lizards and that, if my money were not then available, I would release the lizards in the bank. When I did return two hours later (without any green lizards) I was immediately pointed out to the bank manager as "the lizard man", and he ran into a back room and emerged with all my cash in hand. Had he not produced my money I don't know whether I would have really followed through on my promise fully. I do not believe in idle threats and would surely have shown up with three large male green lizards. On the other hand, the pandemonium and stampede that would have ensued from letting these lizards loose into a bank packed with fifty Jamaicans waiting in long lines for their weekly money might have left me charged that day with multiple counts of manslaughter.

At the bank that day, "lizard man" almost seemed to be a term of honor-bordering-on-terror. But not everyone is positively impressed by my close relationship with lizards. Once, a man riding on the back of a bus caught sight

of me on the road with three or four giant green lizards in hand and shouted out "lizard man" only to have the whole bus shake with laughter. I was
perplexed. It was obvious that I had some kind of special affinity for green
lizards, but why the laughter? I soon learned from my catchers that the man
was suggesting that I'd captured these lizards for sexual purposes! Jesus Christ,
I thought, I know you people think I'm ethnically under-endowed in that
region of my body, but do you have any idea how *small* a lizard's cloaca is?

WHISTLING A MALE GREEN LIZARD INTO SEXUAL PARANOIA

Now that we're on the topic of lizards and sex, this might be a good time
to mention the surprising fact that lizards respond to song even though they
themselves do not sing. A British naturalist noted this more than one hundred
fifty years ago. They also respond to whistling. I discovered this, because I like
to whistle to birds and had tried it out on lizards. A lizard will cock its head
as you start to whistle and may make additional small head movements. The
ear-hole will appear to be slightly larger and darker in color as you whistle,
because, I believe, it orients so as to expose an ear more directly to the sound.

One day I saw a female green lizard perched head down on the trunk of a
large tree at about my level and decided to whistle at her in the style I had developed with birds. That style is to whistle a tune based on some sentences I
am imagining in English. For instance, I might whistle a tune to the sentence,
"You are such a lovely female. What are you doing stuck in a mango tree with
this ugly old male?" The up-and-down pitch of my voice will translate itself
into similar changes in the pitch of my whistles. Whistling in this manner, I
immediately caught the female's attention and she moved ever so slightly in
my direction while cocking her head. I continued to sing to her. Suddenly,
she whirled and ran around the back of the tree, out of sight. I looked up
and saw an enormous male, some twenty feet up the tree, emerging from its
foliage. He was stretched out to his full length and displaying yellowish green,
a green lizard's most aggressive color. His attitude seemed to be, "But a whaa
gwaan here? You a court *my* female?"

TWO PENISES

It is a little known fact outside of Herpetology that all lizard and snake males have two penises, one on the left side and one on the right. A given penis is used preferentially depending on whether the male winds around to the right or the left of the female. (If you are a mammal and have a penis, look down at its underside and see if you do not see a line running up it that shows where the two hemi-penes fused during early development.) Initially in evolution, all genital organs tended to be bi-laterally symmetrical. Testicles and ovaries retained this symmetry, but reductions to one also occurred, as in the case of the penis and the scrotum.

In any case, it is easy to reveal the trait in *Anolis* males. You hold him upside down and manipulate the penis on either side to cause it to extrude. When both are extruded they look like two bananas peeled outwards.

I used to amuse myself by showing this feature off to Jamaican men, knowing that having two penises would arouse excitement, as well as admiration. "One for the yard, one for the road," was a common excited response. Alas, if it were only that easy, I thought to myself. What these men had in mind was segregating the parasites acquired on the road from the sanctity (and knowledge) of the yard, but it was a matter of millimeters for a parasite acquired by the right penis to colonize the left one, so I did not see much safety in this arrangement. Perhaps a better theory for why the lizards have two penises is the benefit of rest between successive encounters. Indeed, research shows that if a male is permitted to rest his right penis for three days it is as good as new. But use it a second time in one day and it produces less sperm than the opposite penis (and testicle). Recently on my property in Jamaica, I saw the largest male copulate from one side at two p.m. and from the opposite at four p.m.

FEMALE CHOICE OR MALE COERCION?

The alternatives were beautifully put many years ago for *Anolis* lizards roughly as follows. Either, "The female is pursued, caught and ravished in the most brutal fashion," or, "Even when running from the male she signals her interest and readiness to copulate." Which is it for green lizards? It is a little bit of both, but mostly female choice. Males attempt to run down females and "ravish them in the most brutal fashion," but they rarely catch them. I have seen a large male suddenly dart six feet down the trunk of a tree, only to watch the female run seven feet up the opposite side of the trunk. She is smaller and more agile – they are in a tree, remember, not on the ground – and her being smaller and more agile pays differential rewards. At the same time, I have seen the same female stand in one place and pose, rear-end slightly raised, full body elevated off the substrate before inviting a somewhat smaller, sleeker and fresher-looking male to approach and copulate. It is easy to assume that a female should prefer the largest male since largeness indicates a healthy ability to grow; but the largest male is also apt to be older. This may account for some of the distaste that females show for the monster males. The biggest are old – and probably ugly, too.

Once I saw a male who had managed to catch a female by the fat section of her tail, close to her body. I saw at once that he had gotten himself into quite an intellectual dilemma. He seemed to know it, too. He acted as if he knew that too hard a bite would cause the tail to break off, leaving him holding the wiggling back end while she ran off. So he held her softly and hunched his back occasionally, as if trying to reach the desired structure while still holding on, but this was physically impossible. He was caught in a hopeless quandary and to watch his little male lizard brain try to solve it, as represented by occasional hunchings of his back, was fun. Eventually, he let go and moved swiftly to cover her but she was now three feet above him and moving rapidly away. Females, being smaller, are faster in trees, so it was truly hopeless from the outset.

Once a neighbor drew my attention to another exciting lizard sexual interaction. A large male regularly copulated with two females on his own tree, and two on a coconut tree ten feet away, while a larger male appeared to look on wistfully from a mango tree twenty feet distant, unable to intervene. In any case, one female on his own tree was slim and probably young and had the unique behavior of raising one leg while copulating, very much as young Jamaican women do when dancing (and, for all I know, while copulating). It was fun to imagine that this young female lizard was giving her male the full human "rub-a-dub" experience.

FALLING INTO A PIT

One spring I returned to studying the coffee lizard, only now with the help of my lizard workers in Southfield. One day we passed by an open water tank, just built, which lacked a lip. That is, people had built a sixteen-foot-square concrete pit fourteen feet deep in the ground to store rainwater but there was no water inside, and they had not built up a few feet of "lip" around the hole, as was common, to increase the size of the tank. Walking by it presented no challenge. But shortly after we'd passed it, one of my lizard men pointed to a large male coffee lizard, which then immediately sprinted toward higher vegetation. This meant that he was a re-capture, a male captured during an earlier visit to the island but not during this one – so his recapture would give us survival and growth rate data. In other words, he was valuable. My three lizard men sprang to the ready – my top man in the fore – climbing the tree in which the lizard was rapidly receding. My job was to keep him in sight so I could help my catchers. I swung my binoculars up, but I was too close – the lizard was not in focus. The proper move in this situation is to walk backwards while keeping the lizard in view; this way he comes into focus without you losing sight of him. Of course you do not wish to do so if two feet behind you is an open pit, which, alas, I had forgotten. I started walking backwards, when suddenly my future brother-in-law (then fourteen years old) called out, "Watch out, Rasta!" and my brain snapped back into focus. I looked down, and saw that I was stepping backwards off the edge toward a fourteen-foot fall onto bare concrete below.

I have practiced the proper move in this situation a hundred times since then – swing your back leg upwards, shift your center of gravity forward, grab the edge of the tank and slide down. Instead, I did the only thing I could to save myself. I kicked off and headed straight down. If the youth had not called out, I would have gone over backwards to my death or at least life-long paralysis. As I plummeted down I planned to take some of the fall on my legs but also to collapse, so as not to take too much pressure on them. As it turned out, I took most of the fall on my right leg and left arm. After landing I felt my bones to see if any was broken, and since none was I stood up (not no-ticing that I had dislocated my right shoulder). I then saw one of the sweetest

FEMALE POSING. Note that the female's body, including entire tail is raised from the substrate, a sure sign, we believe, of sexual interest. (Photo courtesy Robert Trivers.)

sights of my life. Three pairs of eyes simultaneously appeared over the edge of the tank. I knew how they felt. They expected to see me in broken pieces fourteen feet below, their employer and friend either dead or very nearly so, and none wanted to be the first to see the dreadful sight. My greatest lizard catcher even had a sympathy fall, I later learned, from the third branch up the tree to the second when he realized that I had gone over.

As a true post-doc, I asked them if they had caught the lizard. They had not. Since it was obvious I would be in the tank for some time, I suggested they do their work. The lizard was duly caught, tossed down to me, measured, and returned to them before they set about getting me out of the pit. They found a long piece of wood, two clambered down in order to push me up, and one waited at the top to pull me in. With only one working arm, I was hauled out of the pit. Later the good, bald-headed Dr. Campbell in Malvern pulled the classic trick of distracting my attention by telling me to look elsewhere, at which time he suddenly pulled my left arm back into its socket. I was in pain for nine months and I had to sleep on my right side for over a year, but I was alive and in one piece, and that night everyone celebrated my survival by regaling each other with other "falling-in-a-pit" stories.

By the way, the problem of dangerous heights in my life is still with me. The other night, at one in the morning, I turned off the lights in my second floor apartment and headed toward the bedroom in the dark. I walked past the right-hand turn to my bedroom and two feet later turned right into the hallway that led at once to a ten-foot vertical drop in the form of a four-teen-step staircase. For one truly terrifying moment I found myself hurtling, almost head over heels, face down, to what seemed a very unforgiving surface below. One minute you are seeking safety and rest, the next minute you are airborne, with the wrong side of you facing downwards. I lay whimpering at the bottom, flexing my left leg tentatively to make sure it was still in one piece. My girlfriend rushed out of the bedroom to find me with a large gash on my head, blood spurting out. We called 9-1-1, but it did not turn out to be an emergency, only a head gash, no sign of mental dysfunction or other real bodily injury. I crept into my bed and passed out for the night.

THE LIZARD IN ME

I think it is inevitable that after years of studying a particular species or a particular kind of organism you feel a deeper identification and closeness and more of a personal relationship. It is well known that botanists are nicer people than zoologists, invertebrate nicer than vertebrate, and primatologists among the nastiest of all.

Every now and then you feel a kinship with a particular individual. I once grew particularly close to a blue lizard (*Anolis grahami*) that I had trained to share an afternoon's drink with me. This is easy to achieve. Blue lizards like sweet drinks, and if you simply set out one for him at the same time every day he will soon enough search it out. Once he tastes Stone's ginger wine, he

is gone – he wants it every afternoon. Now you both drink together each afternoon. He turns a bright blue-purple-yellow color, which seems in general
to be a sign of arousal and personal happiness. You are turning whatever colors you turn when you drink. The key is that you are in synchrony with the
lizard. Show up at four p.m. and he will be waiting, please bring two glasses.

   This lizard happened to be my drinking companion at a time when I badly needed one. A woman I had loved more deeply than any other for many
years – herself one of the most loving organisms I have ever met – was giving
clear signals that our relationship was over. In my pain, I turned to poetry
and, you can trust me on this, brothers and sisters – as a life-long scientist,
when I am writing poetry, I am in deep pain. Thank God for my lizard friend,
though. Here is the poem I wrote about the two of us:

"We are just friends, man"

We are just friends, man
Blue lizard and me

We meet in the afternoon

You on your perch
Me in my chair

We are just friends, man
Afternoon friends

You like ants
I like sardines

You like your lizard pum-pum
I like mine human

We are just friends, man
Interspecies friends

Do you take pleasure in me
As I in you

Who knows

We are just friends, man
You and me

We are just friends

CHAPTER 5

Tried for Assault Occasioning Bodily Harm

Jamaica is a notoriously violent society, for years having one of the highest murder rates in the world. In the old days, knives, machetes, bottles, and batons might be the weapons of choice, at least in the countryside. About eighteen months into my green lizard work I got involved in something much more minor, a fistfight, but I was duly arrested and tried for assault occasioning bodily harm. Actually I was defending myself from my accuser, a well-known bully, powerfully built, who had initiated the fight by assaulting me.

But this was part of doing research in Jamaica, dealing with one's rural neighbors. There were hardly any all-inclusive hotels back then and, had there been, I would not have been staying at one. Only in Kingston or Ocho Rios or Port Antonio might I spend a night or two in a hotel. I explored the entire island by car using lizards as a pretext and for financial support, but most of the time I was right there in Southfield staying at Miss Nini's home, living in the community and doing my lizard work nearby.

THE FIGHT

One day I received in rural Jamaica my "Dear John" letter from the woman I had loved non-stop since the day I met her as a twenty-year-old undergraduate at Harvard. She made it clear that the relationship was over – over – over! – it was OVER. After a while you got the full pressure of her point; she wanted to make sure that even someone as self-deceived as myself would realize things were over, and she succeeded at that. I thus traveled early to the "back-a-rock" area near Barbary Hall where you could smoke your ganja in reasonable certainty that you would not spend eighteen months in prison at hard labor for doing so. I returned to Miss Nini's home late for my dinner, in a foul mood, and well oiled.

As I was eating, Jasper Bent, Miss Nini's lover, leapt up from the couch and started yelling at her in a very loud and abusive manner. Now, I do not like abuse of women in general, but least of all in my presence, since its continuance implies acquiescence on my part. Miss Nini was a woman in her fifties and someone I loved and respected. As for verbal abuse by others, this is the easiest for me to handle, since I am near the top of the scale where producing a loud and abusive sound is concerned. So I shouted, "Shut your *fucking* rum mouth while I am eating!" As if my mealtime were a holy hour and voices should be muted. In any case, he yelled back, "A who you a talk *so*?" and I jumped up and said, "A *you*!"

He then came through the door separating the small dining area from the living room. He grabbed me and peeled off the front of my shirt, his 220 pounds of well-built farmer hurling me against the wall behind. I bounced off and hit him four or five times, very rapid left jabs, the key punch in keeping a beast at bay. You can finish your attacker off later, if you are lucky, with a right cross, but in the meantime, it is jab, jab, jab, right in his face. In any case it worked, he was driven backwards, and others quickly intervened to separate us. I was so "rahtid" – a Jamaican word for *really* angry – that when I looked down and saw blood on my left hand, I said, "The mother-fucker cut me!" In other words, in hitting him I had cut myself. But even this was not true – the blood was Jasper's. He now bled from the entire right side of his face. My anger was thus so extreme I even projected onto him blame for his blood I had spilled on myself while thumping him.

At that point, I felt confident that the fight was over. I figured he'd seen that I could box and was done with me. Boxing was something I had taught myself at a young age when I was being bullied by bigger, older, stronger boys. At fifteen I had been knocked to the ground in front of a crowd of fellow students, boys and girls alike, because I had talked to the bully's "girl-friend." This was not an experience I wished to repeat so I had snuck into the library and checked out a book by Joe Louis called "How to Box." I started doing push-ups and shadow-boxing according to Joe's instructions and then joined the boxing team at Andover, where I fought for two years. I earned a varsity letter and was a decent boxer, in part because I had to leave my eyes, i.e. my glasses, at ringside. Being near-sighted in a sport in which you would like to quickly spot hostile motions in your direction seemed a clear disad-vantage, and so I learned how to bob and weave, and cover up. But mostly I learned how to use my left jab to keep my opponent at a safe distance in the first place. Exactly what had been required with Jasper.

As it turned out, though, the boxing match was only the beginning of my fight with Jasper. As I was inspecting my hand, I soon heard cries of, "Put down the knife Jasper." I hadn't seen the knife yet, but I yelled, "So you are going to attack me with the knife you stole from me the other day?" "A buy me did buy it," he replied, as indeed he had, but it was curious nonetheless that he had bought my only weapon of self-defense a week before our fight. Curious also that I was so stupid as to give it up. In any case, we each thrust ourselves insincerely at the group of six people separating us. I say "insincere-ly" because either of us could have turned around, run out backwards, and come in behind the other, but neither of us chose to do so.

Next I heard, "Don't do it, Jasper, don't do it," followed by the sounds of my typewriter being mashed up. Right afterward, as I remember it, Jasper drove off. Miss Nini told me she did not think it was safe for me to spend the night in her yard, so I went up to Ma Septy's house and spent the night there with a knife under my pillow. When I walked back down to Miss Nini's shortly after dawn I learned that Jasper had returned at four in the morning, with a police truncheon in hand and had looked high and low for me. I was also advised by Miss Nini to report the matter to the nearest police station in Bull Savannah for my own protection. I did so but was surprised to discover not the slightest interest in my story. No one took notes, and no one paid any attention. I later learned that this was because Jasper had already shown up, and the police were organizing themselves to arrest me.

Returning to Southfield, I felt the matter was getting out of control and that for my safety I should seek out my good friend Ivie, who delivered blocks of ice from his truck every day and, more to the point, carried a licensed firearm. I drove down to his home in Pedro Plains and, as I entered his yard, his wife came running out, yelling at me that I was no longer welcome in her yard and should leave. As of course I did, and stood outside waiting. Then Ivie came to me and asked me what the problem was. I told him and he went and got his firearm and drove with me back to Miss Nini's. As we drove, Ivie explained that his wife, usually so warm and friendly, had only just learned an unfortunate fact about my relationship with him. A couple of times a week, I would pick him up in the evening ostensibly for a drive down to Treasure Beach Hotel for a couple of drinks, surely one of the more boring venues in the parish – nothing but old ("white") people, not a young woman in sight. But we did not, in fact, stop at the hotel. We drove right past it and then onto back, dirt roads that eventually dumped us on the main road we could have reached almost immediately from his home in the opposite direction. Once on the main, we headed down to Barbary Hall, where his girlfriend lived (and also supplied me with a friend). We then later returned to his home by the same back route.

In any case, Ivie and I were now driving back to Southfield when a mongoose started across the road and, upon seeing us, turned back. This is rare. Mongooses are small and very swift and rarely turn back. When it does happen, it is taken as a sign of bad luck. The only logic I can give for this belief is that sometimes we may be going too fast in life, too fast for our own good, and, when we are in that situation on the road, we are more likely to frighten a mongoose into changing its mind and turning back. Whatever the logic, the mongoose puts you on alert – worse is about to come.

When we arrived back in her yard, Miss Nini was looking wild, her hair pointing straight out in all directions and her dark-skinned face shining. She told us that the police had only just left, having arrived in Jasper's own van to arrest me. (They had no other vehicle available.) She also said that Jasper had "pointed out" to the police where I kept an eighty pound crocus bag full of ganja on Nini's front porch, a lie that particularly outraged her. Indeed, within a day she had cut down all the beautiful old vines and flowers covering her porch, the better to make sure that anybody on the road could see that no ganja was stored there. The police left orders for me to appear at the station so I could be arrested for assault.

Ivie and I now set off for the police station, with my battered typewriter in hand as evidence for a counter-charge. I was arrested and made to sit in a room with Jasper opposite me. He did not look happy. The entire right-hand side of his face had been shut down, and his right eye was swollen shut. He looked even less happy when the police reappeared and arrested him for "malicious destruction of property." In fact, he jumped up, outraged, but they took the two of us behind the counter and told us to sit until the detective returned. They claimed we had to wait behind the counter because there was no space in the cells, but I doubt this. My guess is they thought we were too high-class to be treated like common criminals and locked in their nasty cells.

During our arrest, as we waited for the detective to return, a swarm of local people came in and out and observed the two of us from behind the counter. There was a popular song on the island at the time sung by Toots and the Maytals called "One-eye Enos." It featured a man who has lost one of his eyes in a fight, and the question to the attacker is, "What are you going to do, now that you lick out Enos eye, because Enos miss that eye?" Soon enough, men were calling out to Jasper, "Wha happen Enos? How you lose your eye?" Jasper: "The white man lick me with bottle". "Nooooo, man, no white man cyan lick black man so! How you really lose your eye, Enos?" To which of course, he made no reply. Yet they kept it up, hour after hour, and, later, in Southfield as well: "Whaa happen, Enos?"

Ivie, it turned out, was friends with many of the officers and told them around back that this was not as it was made out to be. This was self-defense using fists, not attack using a quart rum bottle. Also, I was a scientist, not a tourist, and much more integrated into Jamaican life than they might have imagined. I believe Ivie was a major reason Jasper was given his matching charge of malicious destruction.

The Lieutenant returned after four hours and asked me what right I had coming to a foreign country and attacking one of its citizens with a quart rum bottle. I leaned forward slightly and said that I had been attacked by this man and had defended myself with fists. I threw two quick jabs for illustrative purposes. He asked who would bail me and Miss Nini stepped forward with Marse Septy, who had vast holdings of land, if not necessarily much money in his pockets. I showed up at court on the following Tuesday and was told to return six weeks later, in early June, for a trial.

THE TRIAL

I returned to Jamaica two days before I was to be tried. I spent a night in Kingston and then drove to Southfield. There I learned that on the night previous, Jasper had been bragging at Connie's bar that he had deported the "Ganja criminal." Which indeed, he would have – in effect – if I had not shown up to face the charges. I would then have faced immediate arrest on return to the island for failing to show up for my trial, an open-and-shut case.

The day of the trial dawned bright and clear, and at six-thirty in the morning Miss Nini, myself, and Little Man set out for the Malvern Courthouse. Little Man was a neighbor, who served as a day laborer and night watchman at the Public Works Department next door to Mrs. Staple's. We arrived in Malvern to find a crowd gathering in the courtyard grounds. Every now and then a lawyer's car would pull up, usually a fancy new model, the window would lower itself a few inches, and a line of people would form to talk through the small opening of the lawyer's slightly ajar window and sometimes pass money inside.

Miss Nini and Little Man were eager to see who Jasper's false witnesses would be. From long knowledge of his behavior, they took it for granted that he would bolster whatever lies he intended to tell by paying for the false testimony of one or more witnesses. For this occasion, it looked as though the Palmer brothers had been pressed into service. Arthur Palmer was a small man in his fifties, dressed in an ill-fitting suit. His brother appeared the same, and neither looked very happy with the job they had been assigned. When Jasper's lawyer arrived, the four of them huddled together for a little chat. We later learned that they were to testify that they had been walking up the road at six in the morning when they saw Miss Nini instructing me on how to mash up my type-writer so as to bring a false case against Jasper.

Little Man watched them with a broad smile on his face and started to bob up and down. "Me can handle dem, Bob, me can handle dem." I asked him what he meant, but he only said, "Don't you worry about nuttin, me can handle dem!" I thought this was just some good ganja talking, or Jamaican bragging, and paid him no mind. We pointed out the false witnesses to Mr. Swaby, my lawyer, a short, light-skinned fellow of about forty years from Mandeville. He did not drive a fancy car and was, in fact, defending me for only sixty dollars.

Cases were tried on the second floor of the courthouse in a large room that was packed with row after row of spectators, many of them there to enjoy what passed at the time for country theatre. There was no electricity then, or television, or much in the way of entertainment of any sort. When my own case was called, my lawyer and I stood facing a judge in robes, a dark-skinned Jamaican man with a goatee, perhaps in his late thirties. He was serious looking and also, as soon became evident, highly intelligent.

As I stood to face the judge, Jasper's lawyer also stood and asked him to collapse each case against the other – in effect, we would each withdraw our charges, and the cases would (in the interests of justice) be dismissed. The judge asked if this was agreeable. No, I protested, I had flown to Jamaica at considerable expense to face these charges and… before I could continue, the judge cut me off. "Your expenses are of no relevance to this matter, and I do not wish to hear any further reference to them." I saw his point, of course, but felt that collapsing the cases would still provide a very unsatisfactory resolution to the matter. I insisted on my right to a trial. To two trials, in fact, mine and his.

So, as requested, I was charged with assaulting Mr. Bent with a quart rum bottle causing him facial cuts. Mrs. Staple (later to become my mother-in-law) turned out to be the key witness. The incident took place in *her* home and our status in her yard was critical to the case. Mr. Bent was a "visitor to the yard" (i.e., he dated Miss Nini) while I was a "guest in the house" (that is, I boarded in the home). I therefore outranked Jasper. In the eye of the law, he was already wrong. I thought this a very sensible bias. If I fight you in your yard, I am already wrong; if you fight me in mine, you are wrong. Of course I could suddenly spring on you unjustly on your property, drag you to the road

MISS NINI. The woman in whose home I boarded, later my mother-in-law, an extraordinary organism head to toe. In that community, me included, she was the brightest, the most honest and the deepest bar none. (Photo courtesy Nola Perez.)

and injure you, and I have heard of such cases decided in favor of the visitor (see below for such a case involving Jasper himself). But status in the yard was critical. It was assumed that we would each, if necessary, manufacture a lie, so priority of residence emerged as an easily verified fact of fundamental significance. Let us, indeed, give a bias toward the homebody, much as herring gulls do in territorial encounters, for they become more nervous the deeper they are dragged into an opponent's area. In the social world of herring gulls, a particularly aggressive move is to grab your opponent and drag him or her *into* your territory.

In any case, Jasper, in his testimony, had attempted to blur this distinction, suggesting that he and Miss Nini were, in effect "common-law" spouses – unmarried lovers living together. But Jasper faced an unfortunate pair of facts: both he and Mrs. Staple were already legally married, and not to each other. Indeed, he was living with his wife. No matter how much time he spent in Miss Nini's yard he could never rise above the status of "visitor to the yard."

I had been planning to tell the court exactly what had happened, as best I recalled, but my lawyer quickly convinced me to make one small change. While I had actually said, "Shut your fucking rum mouth, Jasper," Mr. Swaby felt that, "Shut your rum mouth," was sufficiently faithful to my actual words. "Fucking" is a so-called fighting word, one presumed to induce an almost automatic response – almost as strong as slandering a man's mother. With that word included in my account, my role in inducing my attack loomed larger. Otherwise, I described the encounter exactly the way I remembered it, since the facts were (in my view) all in my favor. In any case, when I had finished my account of Jasper's attack and my defense, the prosecutor asked me how long I had known Mrs. Staple and Mr. Bent. "Six months," I replied. "How long have they known each other?" "I understand twelve years." "Intimately?" he asked. "I *presume* so," I answered and got an unexpected laugh from the audience. "Well how is it that you, knowing these people only six months, would interfere in their dispute when they have known each other intimately for twelve years?" I pointed to Jasper and said, "If I saw this man strangling this woman, I would not ask them how long this relationship has been going on, I would try to stop it."

This reply got an appreciative laugh from the audience and another reluctant smile from the judge. Whatever else, my testimony was thoroughly consistent with stereotype: an American might very well intervene inappropriately in someone else's domestic dispute and, if so, he would certainly use his fists and not a quart rum bottle. By contrast, Jasper and the prosecutor told a thoroughly Jamaican tale of sexual jealousy and intrigue, employing not the weapons of gallantry, but those of wounding and death. Besides the facts of residence, their very difficulty was that one of their actors was not, in fact Jamaican.

Was it really true, as Jasper first reported to the police and now repeated in front of a judge, that he had caught me pushing Miss Nini into her bedroom while asking for "ganja and sex," and intervened on her behalf? And was it really true that I had responded by striking him in the face with a quart rum bottle, thereby wounding him? I had in my favor that the alleged romance between myself and Miss Nini was somewhat implausible on its face. She was twenty-five years my senior. I thought of her as a mother and protected her as same, and people in the neighborhood knew that – she was later to become my mother-in-law.

Incidentally, Jasper may well have believed his own lie about my sneaking behind his back with Miss Nini. His own sexual exploits approached the legendary. Local lore had it that he had once been discovered fooling around with a man's wife in the man's own bed, and jumped out of that bed to beat up the husband for having the gall to walk in on them. Another married woman was known to hang cloth from a tree to signal to Jasper when her mate was nowhere about. In addition to the children by his wife, Jasper was said to have fathered numerous "outside" children. Especially under the influence of alcohol, Jasper was prone to the belief that Miss Nini was treating him as he was treating his wife, keeping lovers secretly on the side. One of his main suspects was always Little Man, a claim that was absurd because, although she and Little Man had a warm and friendly relationship, he was far below Miss Nini in social status, plus short and wiry, not quite the physical specimen she preferred. Miss Nini, anyway, was disinclined to see more than one man at a time and lacked completely the dishonesty necessary to keep multiple affairs running smoothly.

That one's own misconduct makes one suspect similar misconduct by others, even where none exists, strikes me as an agreeable feature of life, a kind of unexpected return tax on an originally selfish act. Jasper's long enjoyment of faithless women had apparently rendered him unable to recognize the love of a faithful one. I can still amuse myself wondering how the easy warmth and familiarity of Nini with Little Man must have tortured Jasper's rum-inflamed imagination

Finally, the judge almost mumbled the words "not guilty," looking down a bit wistfully, undoubtedly regretting the time lost in trying such a minor case. I sat down, and Jasper now stood up, accused of malicious destruction of property — one typewriter and one t-shirt. I was now a witness for the prosecution. After identifying the items, I told how he had first torn up my shirt and then destroyed my typewriter. Under cross-examination, I admitted that I had not *seen* the typewriter destroyed but had merely heard shouts of "Jasper, put down that typewriter!" followed by sounds such as a typewriter, being destroyed, might make.

JASPER'S FALSE WITNESS

Mrs. Staple gave similar testimony except that she claimed actually to have *seen* the typewriter being destroyed. The prosecution rested and Jasper's defense began. Immediately, they called one of the false witnesses, Arthur Palmer, to the stand. Nobody stirred. Again Arthur Palmer's name was called out, and again nobody responded. Jasper spun around and searched the crowd with his eyes. His lawyer spun around. They conferred heatedly, and then Jasper's lawyer, Mr. July from Black River, told the judge that he had good assurances that Mr. Palmer had, indeed, come to court to testify and asked that a bailiff be dispatched to the balcony to call to the crowd below.

"Arthur Palmer! Arthur Palmer!" boomed the bailiff's voice from the balcony, but not a soul stirred. "Arthur Palmer! Arthur Palmer!" Wherever he was, Arthur had no intention of appearing. Nor did the second witness. Jasper's case collapsed. He was quickly found guilty of malicious destruction of property, and forced to pay me US$80. As we left Malvern Court House we could see Jasper harshly berating the Palmer brothers, who were looking at their shoes.

It took Little Man to explain what had happened. He had taken the Palmer brothers for a drink and while buying them white rum (152 proof) had explained the situation to them. This was not a simple case such as they were used to. This was Jasper against the *white man*. The judge might well imprison *them* for their false witness, which was unheard of in a typical case. Meanwhile, he bought each man another shot of white rum. When their names were finally called, Little Man assured us, they well heard them, indeed each bowed his head as if to let his name roll harmlessly overhead. A good old Ganja-head like Little Man (stone cold sober) manipulated two rum heads with ease – combining fright with inebriation to bring about the right states of mind.

As we passed through Southfield, we repeatedly hit the car horn in cele-bration. According to Miss Nini, Jasper had been involved in ten prior court cases and had lied his way to success in all of them. He was, in fact, a noto-rious bully, backed by two equally sizable brothers. In one case, Jasper had seized a man on the man's own property, dragged him out onto the road, and beaten him with a rock. I'd heard his own account of the crime in Miss Nini's living room. Jasper had told it with his face alight, arms outstretched, the more vividly to recapture the moment. He claimed he had been walking innocently down the road, when this man, cursing him, had leapt from his own yard and swung a machete at him. Every man's nightmare: an unpro-voked, surprise attack with a lethal weapon! Jasper had, in an instant, grabbed the man's arm and staved off the blow until the machete only grazed the back of his skull. Then Jasper leapt forward, his eyes aglow as he grabbed the arm and machete, and skillfully deflected all except a glancing blow. He had held the man down on the road and given him a couple of good fists in the face, the better to cure him of such misbehavior.

I remember myself leaning forward, eyes aglow, as I imagined that I was, at that moment, almost an actual eyewitness to an anthropologically significant event. A just man skillfully deflects a surprise attack at close quarters and, in his grandeur, returns only fists for machete! And yet I could also hear Miss Nini's voice in the background saying, "Nuttin nuh go so Bob, nuttin nuh

go so!" And, of course, as I later learned, nothing *did* go so. Jasper's story was
a lie, from beginning to end, the original indictment was valid, and yet Jasper
was not only acquitted of assault, he was congratulated by the judge and told
that he, Jasper, should, in fact, have beaten the man with a rock – as he had,
in fact, done.

JASPER ATTACKS LITTLE MAN

One late afternoon, about three months after the court case, when I was off
the island, Little Man was enjoying a drink at Connie's shop when Jasper,
with four or five of his day laborers (men who worked in his fields and were
paid by the day), arrived on the scene. All immediately set upon Little Man
and beat him to the ground. Little Man got to his feet and told them that he
might be a rooster (a small man) but it was some tough old fowl meat they
were dealing with, and if they thought they could handle him "so" (that is,
with no other consequence) they were sadly mistaken.

He went next door, to the part of the shop, where groceries were sold, and
ordered a few items. These he paid for but, in his haste to depart, he (apparently) left them behind. Returning to his house, he put a knife in his back
pocket and returned shortly to retrieve his "forgotten" groceries. Arriving to
pick them up, he decided to stop for an apple juice and ordered a tin. While
drinking the juice, he stood with his back to the counter, and leaned casu-
ally against it. Almost immediately one of Jasper's men spotted Little Man
through a small window that connected the bar and the grocery store and
called out, "See Little Man deya!"

Jasper flew around the corner and rushed to attack, but Little Man was
ready. He crouched low, reached for his knife, and thrust it into Jasper's on-
rushing bulk, aiming it straight for the heart. The knife, however, was a relatively thin kitchen knife, and as it struck a rib just above the heart it snapped.
The remaining stub made an ugly wound and blood spurted from Jasper's
chest, but the wound was entirely superficial. His heart was safe.

There was, of course, a hullabaloo: shouting, screaming, blood spurting
from Jasper's chest, and so on. Connie closed his shop, the better to avoid a

death therein. Jasper, in his fury, drove straight to Bull Savannah to have Little Man arrested, but Little Man had his own plans. He returned to his yard with a friend. He found an empty quart rum bottle and broke it against a rock. He handed it to his friend and instructed him to rake Little Man's belly a couple of times with the jagged edges of the broken bottle. His friend did as told, so that when the police arrived later that night they found Little Man bleeding from his side, in obvious pain, and with quite a different story to tell about the evening. How Jasper first attacked him with a broken bottle and how, during the second such attack, he desperately defended himself, using only a kitchen knife.

The police carried both men to Black River Hospital to be treated for their injuries and then arrested and charged each man with one count of wounding. Later, the two cases were collapsed against each other, i.e., both charges were dropped in court. Injuries were equivalent on both sides and so were charges, so the men agreed, in effect, to forget about it, and the state withdrew its interest in the matter.

It is worth taking a moment to consider — indeed, admire — Little Man's achievement. He had already served eleven months in prison for wounding. He would have been dealt with very harshly for a repeat offense against a solid citizen, perhaps ten years at hard labor. He had, in fact, fully intended to kill Jasper, he assured me later, and had only taken the kitchen knife because no other knife was at hand. He felt certain that Jasper would attack him again if he had the nerve to reappear so soon (and nonchalantly) at the scene of his recent beating. In the harshest light, Little Man's crime was attempted murder, carefully premeditated, and out of a motive of revenge. Yet his only overt act was to make himself available for further abuse and his attempt at murder did not begin until he was moments away from being attacked. The beauty of the deception is obvious. Little Man bought groceries in order to have something to forget, for which he had to return, thus hiding the premeditation of going for a knife. His relaxed posture while he enjoyed an apple juice was also meant to infuriate Jasper while hiding his own violent intentions.

And yet it is still so often not considered "fair," after the fact, for a small man to use a knife to defend against the fists of a big man. But Little Man's considerable powers of deception evened the conflict.

ME SAY "THAT BOB IS A SHIT"

My final encounter with Jasper occurred perhaps six months after our fight. I walked into Connie's bar and walked past Jasper, turned a corner, and stood next to his brother Ton-Ton, who was, if anything, the stronger of the two. I ordered a drink. Jasper said in a loud voice, punctuated by a loud pounding at the bar, "Me say dat Bob is a shit!" I said nothing and enjoyed my drink. Again: "Me say Bob is a shit," fist crashing down. Now his brother and others intervened verbally. "Nuh bodder wid dat, Jasper." Then Ton-ton wanted us each to buy the other a drink, a little make-up session I have never chosen to participate in. Why? Jasper and I are friends now? He attacks me, destroys my property, comes looking for me the next morning with a police baton, lies in court, and brings paid liars with him. Why should we be friends? I enjoyed my drink by myself and left.

Looking back now on my interactions with Jasper, I see how our conflict at once induced complex processes of deception, counter-deception, and self-deception more powerful and interesting than the original fight. So along with a high value put on violence in Jamaica, there was also high value on dishonesty. This is — as has been argued by others — a general feature of the tropics. There are far more frequent social interactions, thus more opportunities for attendant deceit and self-deception. In any case, seeing the tactical value of deception firsthand made me relax my moral and moralistic aversion to it. This permitted me to study it more freely, which helped when I later wrote a book on the subject.

CHAPTER 6

The Death of Flo

I had the good fortune of befriending Irven Devore, the celebrated baboon man, even before I reached Harvard. He was employed by the same educational company that gave me my first job. The National Science Foundation paid to have superb baboon footage shot in Kenya under DeVore's guidance, so I spent many afternoons watching raw footage that he'd narrated in order to help guide the film in their editing. In watching this footage, what was at once apparent was that baboons were highly social, highly intelligent creatures, often acting out very complex social dynamics. DeVore's narrations helped underscore this fact.

DeVore, incidentally, was one of the greatest lecturers I have ever heard. Take one of his patented great inventions, used in lecture and conversation alike. If in talking with him, you would say, "To make a long story short" he would hold up his hand and say, "No, Bob, when you get to that phrase, the story has already gone on too long, and you must say instead 'to make a long story *shorter.*'" This invariably gets a laugh from classroom and friend alike – and puts us all on the same side.

Of course he didn't always give a good lecture, and Harvard undergraduates back then were remarkably unforgiving. While they didn't come right out and boo, they did hiss. After one miserable lecture, complete with hisses and groans and, in fact, no visible progress in the talk itself, we teaching fellows left the hall huddled close to Irv for mutual protection, Irv would say amiably yet clearly, "Another case of casting false pearls before real swine." We all chuckled, and I thought, is there nothing that disturbs this man? Nothing he can't overcome?

When I was his graduate student teaching fellow, Irv provided me office space and I had access to him in the late afternoons. As he did his paperwork, he would often share with me some part of the inner workings of Harvard. "Here, take a look at this," he would say and pass me some confidential memo that was either revealing, amusing, or both. I taught him social theory based on natural selection, which came as a revelation to him, having been raised on the group selection fallacy of social anthropology. It took him about six months, but once he got it he got it. He taught me monkeys and apes, hunter-gatherers, how to be a better lecturer, and some of the inner workings of a university bureaucracy.

We became hard and close friends. Many an evening would be spent drinking and talking at his home into the wee hours. When I was a post-doc, Irv had some extra research money and proposed a two-month jaunt through several major primate sites, langur monkeys in India, baboons and other big mammals throughout East Africa, and chimpanzees in a remote region of Tanzania.

ALL-MALE LANGUR TROOPS

Our first visit was to India to two sites where Hanuman langurs were being studied, one an Indian site in Jaipur, where S. M. Mohnot reigned, the other a Harvard site in Mt. Abu, where Irv's student Sarah Hrdy held sway. Perhaps because they are sacred in the local Hindu religious groups, langurs are allowed to roam through village and countryside unmolested. Langurs are unusual in that "bi-sexual" troops typically have only one adult male and up to fifteen adult females with their progeny. Given an initial 1:1 sex ratio, the typical troop make-up means there are a lot of males living without females, indeed living in all-male troops. At the time, we were primarily studying bi-sexual troops, but one day we ran across an all-male troop, consisting of about twenty fully adult males and perhaps eight sub-adults. An unhappier set of organisms I have never seen in my life. The pack seethed with tension and aggression, males continually threatening each other while walking in a stilted, aggressive fashion, sometimes culminating in mounting another male, with no evidence of erection, penetration, nor enjoyment on either side. This was a clear downside to living in a society with a sex ratio badly biased against you, and I was glad I belonged to a different species and society.

It is even worse for langur infants. When a new male takes over a bi-sexual troop, he murders off all dependent infants as well as all those born in the next five months – none of whom could have been sired by him, and all of whom inhibit future maternal reproduction with him. In many areas of India, ten percent of langur infants of every generation perish through male infanticide. Most anthropologists in the early 1970s embraced the group selection theory that male infanticide of infants is a nifty population regulation device. It is no such thing. There is no correlation between density of monkeys and frequency of infanticide, but there is a very strong correlation of infanticide with recent male take-over. Infanticide is a device selected in males to advance narrow personal reproduction at the cost of babies and their mothers. It was hideous to hear described and to see in photos, but Irv and I never saw any, it only lay all around us.

THE DEATH OF FLO

As part of our seven weeks in East Africa in the summer of 1972, we took a two-hour boat ride across Lake Tanganyika from Kigoma in order to reach the famous Gombe Stream Reserve. The Reserve was a series of base camp buildings on the shore of the lake, and student sleeping quarters dotting the hills, within which roamed chimpanzees, three groups of baboons, and some leopards.

Within a couple of hours, Irv and I stood with Jane Goodall and her husband Hugo Van Lawick, watching Flo and her son Flint on the hillside among some trees. Flo was the most famous living chimpanzee, having been studied by Jane for more than ten years. She was a matriarch whose clan had formed the backbone of Jane's writings and films. Flo was far past her prime when I saw her and, in fact, was afflicted with continual diarrhea. As we watched, she took a fruit and tried to smash it against a tree but she missed and struck her own leg. "I have never seen her miss like that," said Jane. "I don't give her two weeks to live." My young post-graduate heart leapt. I had just arrived for a two-week visit. According to Jane I would be witness to history!

Jane knew her chimpanzees. Several days later I was watching a "waterfall display," in which chimpanzees, especially adult males, work themselves into a frenzy in the presence of a waterfall, swinging back and forth on vines, hooting, hair erected, and so on. One can almost see, but not quite define, a religious sentiment, an elemental force on which later might be built something as huge as the Catholic Church.

In any case, while our chimpanzees were starting to work themselves up, we were interrupted by the arrival a third student with the shocking news that Flo was dead. I was with two graduate students at the time, and we turned, as if one, and padded back down the paths toward the hillside near the base camp. Turning off the main path, we went through undergrowth and reached the bank of the small river that flowed down toward camp. Flo lay half in the water. Next to her knelt Jane. And capturing this moment for posterity was one of the largest cameras I had ever seen, on a tripod with Hugo behind the lens, just across the river. Flint, meanwhile, lay depressed in a tree twenty feet above his mother.

Thus began the *human* drama of Flo's death. At the beginning, Jane appeared intent upon seeing a chimpanzee funeral. At the very least she hoped that one or more of Flo's grown children might happen upon the body and give some interesting reaction. In fact, it never happened. Instead, the first night Flo remained where she'd died, but Jane sat up the whole night nearby, with many of us for company, in order to deter scavengers such as bush pigs from carting off Flo's carcass (one reason one would not expect to see many chimpanzee funerals). Jane was nostalgic, remembering the early days, nearly alone with the chimpanzees, enjoying the quiet beauty of the forest, coming to know Flo almost as well as her own mother.

In the morning, a discreet watch was kept on the body, but no chimpanzees (other than Flint) encountered it. That evening Flo's body was carried down to the base camp and placed in a room next to Irv's, a room with shared air space. The next day Irv complained to me not so much about spending the night with a cadaver, but about the fact that Flo's body was then carted back

LANGUR FEMALES ATTACKING AN INFANTICIDAL MALE. The females are friends, they are trying to prevent the murder but they are not successful. Later, as Hrdy showed, the females switched roles. (Photo courtesy Sarah Hrdy.)

up to its original resting place, with half of the body in the river. Since our drinking water was taken downstream from that river, Irv could see no reason why Flo couldn't have been returned to within a meter of her actual death spot, with the body *outside* the water. After all, Jane had already interfered with the natural order by protecting the body from scavengers on two successive nights. Why strive now for trivial verisimilitude when we may thereby be putting our own health on the line?

Jane's special relationship with Flo's body continued. A Tanzanian vet from Kigoma was sent for in order to perform an autopsy, but when he arrived he was kept waiting and then told there would be no autopsy after all. Jane would not treat the body as a mere scientific specimen when it was that of a dear and much-mourned friend, in fact her chimpanzee mother. The vet returned to Kigoma the next day.

But he was to return, for, curiously enough, Flint died several weeks later. As he had been seen tasting his mother's diarrhea before she died, a parasite in common was at least a possible explanation. Of course the failure to autopsy

AN INFANT VICTIM. The langur youngster is dead by morning. (Photo courtesy Sarah Hrdy.)

Flo now precluded a direct comparison with Flint's death. Flint's autopsy suggested that he'd died from a gastrointestinal infection of unknown origin.

In her response to the death of a member of a closely related species, Jane Goodall revealed the curious ambivalence we display toward the dead bodies of members of our own species. It is as if the decaying body too sharply erodes the living memory for us to leave it alone. Yet from the standpoint of parasites alone, we surely should: any living creature carries a number of parasites and may have died from an ongoing parasite attack. The parasites can be expected to flee the dead body in search of living tissue. If any are there, they should swarm out of a corpse.

This at once suggests the value of burial if one isn't going to opt for immediate incineration, common in some tropical regions. From the archaeological record we know that humans have practiced this custom for at least seventy five thousand years. But a sentimental component shows up from the beginning, as well, since even in ancient burials the deceased is interred along with various artifacts, such as utensils, weapons, and other items of value. Recently, a Mafia don's burial crypt was shown to contain bones of multiple unidentified individuals – perhaps victims or "friends."

Imagine that it was Jane's own human mother who had died. Why not do an autopsy if this were of any use? We were dealing with a corpse here, not a person. Here Jane had invested more than a dozen years in a chimpanzee female for scientific purposes and she suddenly decided that the corpse was unworthy of such analysis because she had a personal relationship with its previous owner. This really underscored for me just how strangely we relate to the hunks of organic matter that once held people.

The effects of a lingering memory are notoriously strong in various monkey mothers for their recently dead offspring; in some species they carry around the body of an infant in a clinging posture for as long as two days after its death. A much stronger attachment occurs in our own species, as when the exact spot of burial is preserved in memory, often with a marker, so that the desecration of such places by others is taken as an attack on the living relatives. Consider the outrage that recent attacks on Jewish cemeteries have evoked. The attackers, who dug up corpses and assaulted some of these, were regarded as more depraved and anti-Semitic than those who do harm

to living Jews, as indeed they may be since if they are that eager to dese-
crate burial grounds, God knows what else they are eager to do. Or consider
President Carter who responded to the sight of a mullah kicking one of the
American corpses, dead in an accident of his own ill-conceived rescue operation, by decrying the mullah's lack of humanity.

There's something deeply irrational about our reaction to corpses, and the
example of monkey mothers toting around their tiny dead tells us that this
irrational reaction runs deep in our history. And though I can stand back as a
scientist and see it for what it is in others - irrational - I must confess that if I
caught someone unearthing my Aunt Mary's remains and exposing them to
general view, I would probably be seized by anger as well — why should her
remains be subject to public view? She was *my* Aunt Mary.

CHIMPANZEE DECEPTION

Chimpanzees are highly practiced at deception. Many, many examples have
been described from nature and in the lab. Here is a humble example from
my own life. One day two chimpanzee females left camp with their infants.
They were followed by five scientists. Since I ranked lowest, I was fifth and
last in line. After a while, the chimpanzees left the path we were walking
along and turned into the undergrowth. At first we had to duck down under branches, then we were crawling on all fours, finally we were slithering
on our bellies. There were now four sets of feet between the chimpanzees
and me, so I decided to turn back. When I reached where I could crawl I
was surprised to come face-to-face with one of the three female chimps we
had been following. Indeed, she looked equally surprised to see me. She had
apparently deliberately taken us through ever-denser vegetation in order to
make it easy to lose all of us by simply doubling back. Which is apparently
exactly what she and her friend did. I returned to camp knowing my viewing
opportunities were over for the morning, but so were those of my partners.
They returned almost three hours later, having spent the entire time trying
to find the chimps, one of whom I was the last to see.

PARENTAL DISCIPLINE IN BABOONS

One day at Gombe I saw what appeared to be a baboon family acting in a very human way. An adult female, with an infant of about five months and a young juvenile of about two years, sat under a tree, closely attended by an adult male, who groomed her. Adult male baboons are formidable animals, with huge canine teeth, and are the size of very large dogs. They weigh more than two times what adult females weigh. Their very presence provides protection from external enemies while threatening other baboons as well.

In any case, the juvenile was playing with its sibling when the infant reared up on its hind legs and lost its balance, falling over backward. It started to right itself, like a turtle, when its flailing arms caught the attention of the adult male. He took one look over at the juvenile – who immediately scampered up a nearby tree – and then strode over to the tree. The tree, alas, was only about six feet tall and the male reached up and grabbed the juvenile, shook him twice and dropped him.

The scene immediately brought to mind images of adult discipline in baboons as seen through the eyes of Irv DeVore and recorded on film: dominant adult males rushing across the savannah to grab an offending juvenile, shake and sometimes mock-bite the individual on its neck, usually in response to signals of distress from a smaller and younger animal. In this case, the juvenile had not even been in the wrong – it only looked that way. His consciousness of his predicament was sufficiently developed that he thought immediately to take evasive action. This seemed remarkably similar to the rule underlying similar situations in humans: I don't care who is right or wrong, you are older, so I will hold you responsible and punish you.

It thus seemed obvious that as much as parent-offspring conflict had to do with parental resources (milk or parental attention) in monkeys, at least it also had to do with parental manipulation of the offspring's social tendencies. The conflict could in principle affect the offspring's personality for parental benefit long after the parents were dead and gone. These kinds of conflicts seem to be an inevitable consequence of the imperfect degrees of relatedness that connect the various individuals. Parents are equally related to each of their offspring and are expected to value increments in their offspring's welfare

BABOON DISCIPLINE. A male mock-bites a juvenile for misbehaving, then casts him or her aside. (Photo courtesy Irven DeVore.)

(=reproductive success) equally. But each offspring is related to a full sibling by only half, while being fully related to itself, so it is expected to devalue costs to siblings by half when comparing them to benefits to self. In other words, siblings aren't going to treat each other as well as the parents want them to treat each other.

That the offspring's very conscience and personality could be at stake in disciplining was a revelation to me, one with profound implications, including a new theory for the function of self-deception. Clearly both parent and offspring were selected to deceive each other and, when possible, to hide the deception by first denying it to self and then to others. I am doing this for your benefit not mine, this hurts me as much as it hurts you, and so on. At the same time, the offspring had to deal with the problem of induced self-deception, tempted, or even forced, to believe a lie that serves parental interests, rather than its own. These observations ignited a small brainstorm in me that lasted for a few weeks, after which my parent-offspring conflict paper was finished, and I had the first plausible theory for the function of self-deception. The idea was that self-deception evolved in order the better to deceive others.

During the same East African trip, we drove to the Mara-Masai reserve to visit a long-term study of baboon behavior the better to check in on their latest findings. Irv was immediately dismayed by the fact that the current U of California graduate student studying this troop now for eighteen months, based on two years prior work, could still only identify by sight about two-thirds of the baboons he was now studying at a safe distance of some two hundred meters. This was hardly what Irv thought of as updating himself on baboon behavior. Within a day, he took over the project. He got the graduate student to let him drive the Land Rover, and within a couple of hours we were driving through the troop – the graduate student hopefully overwhelmed with data – while Irv pointed out that that the eight-month old juvenile on the right was vomiting and looked sickly while the one on the left, striding next to what looked like his dominant mother, looked fit and ready. The view from the inside is always the deeper view.

HUNTING WITH HUNTING DOGS

The following two anecdotes involve neither Irv Devore nor baboons, but I am including them here because they are interesting stories that involve observation of animals in Africa.

In 1978 I joined my graduate student James Malcolm on the Serengeti Plains in Tanzania. He was already an authority on the dog family, and he was studying hunting dogs, which are not closely related to our kinds of dogs. These had an unusual social system in which typically only one couple bred, and brothers or other male relatives of the father acted as helpers at the nest, as did an occasional relative of the mother. Our task was to find out if their behavior fit Hamiltonian expectations – that is, whether these helpers gained more genetically than they would have through personal reproduction.

The dogs went out at night to hunt as a group, often bringing down sizable prey such as a wildebeest or a small antelope. They then gobbled up as much as they could, and (when reproducing) returned to the home den and regurgitated much of the food to the pups. James was trying to measure the whole thing, intake, output and, if possible, who was related to whom.

The most fun we had was living together for several days in a Land Rover, during which we followed the dogs every night without returning to the research camp. We had plenty of food and fuel and we slept during the day in two hammocks slung side by side in the Rover. We had an afternoon breakfast together and then followed a particular dog pack when it went out hunting. At first, the dogs loped along and were easy to follow, but as soon as they spotted prey and took off after them, the pace picked up sharply. Now we were speeding at thirty to forty miles an hour across the weld, with very limited visibility and over terrain with numerous hedgehog holes and other holes large enough to take off a wheel or even break an axel. Our goal was to arrive at the kill as quickly as we could so that James could measure the consumption of the prey by the different dogs, hopefully followed later by measures of the food being regurgitated by these same dogs to the pups.

There was only one little hitch. Hyenas also liked to arrive at hunting dog kills as soon as possible, the better to consume the prey themselves. Whenever they saw dogs streaking across the plains, they usually took off in hot pursuit, but they often failed to see the dogs. Not so for James' Land Rover. It was large, stood high off the ground and, best of all, had two bright headlights. So the hyenas cued on his Land Rover and all three of us arrived that first night within moments of each other. Two hyenas were already in a pitched battle with the dogs, trying to grab the prey or portions of it for their own consumption. Although badly outnumbered and vulnerable to attacks on their flanks, hyenas are large and dangerous animals, as the hunting dogs well knew.

The hyenas were threatening to eat James' PhD thesis, something he was not inclined to allow. Suddenly James entered the fray on the side of his dogs. He repeatedly drove the Land Rover straight at a hyena, causing it to retreat, then backed up and charged the other one. Back and forth, he fought to keep the hyenas at bay while a few of the dogs harried them from behind and the rest consumed the prey. Meanwhile James started keeping notes on which dogs were swallowing how much meat. His interventions seemed successful

OFFSPRING DISCIPLINE OF MOTHER. My daughter Natasha about to slap her mother, Lorna, whose look suggests that this would not be a good idea. Natasha did not follow through. (Trivers File Photo.)

– most of the kill ended in the bellies of the killers and the hyenas got relatively little for their troubles. We then followed the dogs at a much more leisurely pace back to their own camp in order to quantify regurgitation of food to the pups.

On the way back, I couldn't help myself. I was after all, his thesis advisor. In my gentlest tone, I said, "James, how exactly are you going to handle what I just saw in the methodology section of your thesis?" There was a short laugh and a long pause (or perhaps the other way around). The best that could be said about his situation was that he had created an artificial problem with his highly visible Land Rover and had attempted to correct for the problem using the same Land Rover, but you had to see the scene at the kill – James versus hyenas – to fully appreciate the absurdity of gathering scientifically pure data in the wild. I don't remember seeing anything about it in the methodology section of his thesis, nor being distressed by its omission.

PELICAN COOPERATIVE HUNTING IN SENEGAL

In the northeastern corner of Senegal, near the famous city of St. Louis, is the largest marshland preserve in the world, indeed the third largest bird preserve anywhere. It is a glorious intersection of marine and freshwater – two rich worlds colliding and intertwining. Traveling with a boatman and a local naturalist, I saw large snakes (longer than me) swim by our motorboat with ease. I saw an act of natural selection when my guide pointed to a rapid takeoff of white (adult) pelicans from their breeding island while a fox grabbed a brown chick, too slow on the uptake.

My guide also showed me the most beautiful display of all. Under the right conditions (whatever these were) the pelicans would form a large circle, everyone facing inwards, perhaps thirty or forty pelicans. They would then lean backwards and paddle their feet underneath while moving inwards, thus tightening the circle, including any fish. Suddenly in response to some unseen signal, they dove into the water in unison in order to maximize the number of fish they grabbed up. Watching this huge cooperative spectacle, my heart went out to the thoroughly frightened fish below.

CHAPTER 7

Robbed at Gunpoint in East Kingston

In the late 1960s you used to be able to find a very pleasant club in East Kingston, just past the insane asylum on Windward Road. For a traveling man, in town for short periods of time, the Village Club offered some distinct advantages: besides a bar and dance floor, it rented out rooms for the night and also separately housed several young women whom you could meet in the bar and dance area.

For a reasonable sum of money (say, US$80), you could drink, dance, rent yourself a room and, more than likely, spend the night with a young lady. You were, of course, thereby encouraging prostitution and about this you felt some guilt, but not enough to keep you from coming. In the early days I became friends with the woman who ran the establishment on behalf of unseen owners. She was perhaps like a madam. She ran the bar and booked the rooms. She also directed the girls. She was white and thin, with black-dyed hair and a heavily-painted face. She was perhaps in her mid-fifties, and she lived on the premises. Her boyfriend was a strong, stout, dark-skinned Jamaican man perhaps in his mid-forties. There were two or three other male employees, men who acted primarily as bartenders.

It was an advantage that the club was somewhat off the beaten trail, located at the end of a dead-end street in a residential area not well travelled by the general public. On the other hand, its isolation also posed a threat. You could be robbed or hurt and, in an indifferent or even hostile neighborhood, it might take some time to raise an alarm. I was always conscious of this as I travelled up the street toward the club. For one thing, I always took care, before stopping at the club, to turn my car around so it was facing away, the better for a quick getaway. The club had a high, walled exterior and was surrounded by a wall and a fence. You entered through a door, which had a narrow window permitting you to see into the club and to be inspected, in turn, from within the club. Initially left open, in later years the door was locked and you had to knock to enter. In any case, once you stepped through you found yourself inside a compound: walled in on all sides, containing various back rooms and walkways, including a dance area and a bar directly to your left and, in the '70s, a country kitchen under thatch in an open area to the right. Even in the late '60s, the back was closer to the surrounding neighborhood, a shorter fence, for example, so that you were conscious that if ever the neighborhood were to come crashing into you it would probably come over the back fence.

After ganja was decriminalized by the government in the mid-'70s, it was sold out back. This corresponded with the appearance of some young men from the nearby community who also may have had some association with the resident workers. This was fully consistent with a larger change occurring throughout the island. Jamaicans were reclaiming their beaches, so that hotels, for example, could no longer exclude the larger population from prime stretches of North coast shoreline. As reggae and Rasta culture captured song and dance, country dances at the shop pesa were increasingly populated by rural Rastas – and pseudo-Rastas such as myself. The male newcomers at the Village Club came, as expected, over the back fence.

In 1974 I got married and stopped visiting the Village Club for several years. In December 1978 a colleague was visiting from the United States so I took him to the club, along with Jamaican friends from the countryside. My friend from the U.S. immediately noticed that we were entering a compound at the end of a dead-end road. He was not reassured by the sight of several hostile-looking young men in the dance area. Nor was I by the behavior of a young woman who enticed me into a back room but wanted to leave me there in order to consult with others. When they were unable to exchange US$50 for a proper amount of Jamaican, I seized on this pretext to escape, saying I would return when I had changed the money. My American friend, a professor from the University of California, was delighted to be in the car speeding away from the club. So, it turned out, were my Jamaican friends. One had approached an Indian woman and been rebuffed. After leaving him alone to sit with a somewhat malevolent-looking Jamaican man in his late twenties she returned, all smiles, to solicit his companionship – a turn of events he correctly found ominous.

I JOIN AN ARMED ROBBERY IN PROGRESS

I tried to visit the club twice in 1979 but each time a taxi driver outside my hotel, the Sheraton in New Kingston, said that he would not take me there because, "The club gone bad." One night in October I found myself in a rented car returning from a club in Rae Town, near where the General Penitentiary is located in East Kingston, and some spirit seized me and I turned sharply up Windward Road and said to myself, "Let's see how bad bad is." I was about to find out.

As I parked my car, facing outward, and stepped up to the door, an unusual thing happened. A young woman stepped out of the shadows and asked if I wished to go into the club. This had never happened before and, as it was obvious that I was walking right toward the club door, with no other alternative in sight, I wondered what was going on. But not enough to be put on guard. I said, "Yes," and she proceeded to press against the window and knock. After a short delay, the door was opened and she walked in "winding up her bottom," the better to rivet my attention. Immediately I was seized on both sides by two men, each of whom stuck a revolver just behind my ear and pushed me forward. To the left, with his back to the wall at the dance floor, stood a medium-sized dark-skinned Jamaican man in his forties. He was holding his forehead, where there appeared to be a wound dripping blood into a puddle on the floor. I must confess when I first saw the blood I thought it was catsup. I knew I had blundered into a fleecing operation and that the next several minutes were not going to be pleasant, but at first I thought it was a show, a little urban theatre created to frighten me out of my money. Make-believe. I was soon disabused of this notion. Besides the two holding guns on me, there were three more gunmen, one watching the injured Jamaican and two waiting to greet me. All were young, in their late teens and early twenties, and all seemed nervous and highly agitated.

"WHERE DE MONEY DEH?"

Immediately the two men I was facing began yelling, "Where de money deh? Where de money deh?" and began searching my pockets. I turned slightly to the right, the better to permit access to my wallet on my back left, but as if operating on the opposite premise they searched *away* from the direction I was turning. They quickly found $35 Jamaican in loose bills (about US$10), my hotel key and my car keys. Then the leader said, "Up against the wall." I could see the Jamaican man with his back to the wall bleeding from a head wound, probably from a gun-butting, so I decided to protect my face and reveal my wallet. I moved face up against the wall with my hands on the wall. At that very moment, some other fool wishing to join the party knocked on the door and the leader motioned the two men guarding me to let him in. They did so, placing their guns once again to his head and rushing him forward to be searched. "Where de money deh? Where de money deh?" I could hear as I looked toward the door.

I could see at a glance that the door was not locked from the inside. In the past I had sometimes awakened in the morning without sufficient cash to pay my bar bill. I had then slipped out to return later. This, in turn, led the people to lock the door on me from the inside. To avoid embarrassment I had learned to tell at a distance if the door was already locked. I could see now that it was not. So I decided to make my move. Hell or high water, this was my chance. I dashed to the door, threw it open, and stepped out to my freedom.

I MAKE GOOD MY ESCAPE

The rent-a-car stood to my right but was useless. Even if I had had the keys I would not have stopped to get inside. I turned left and took off running down the street. I felt strong and free no longer penned up in a compound gone bad, and I had no intention of being captured again that night. They could chase me to Spanish Town, I was not coming back. Halfway down the street at curbside was a crowd of Jamaicans I had noticed on the way up. Since none of them had signaled to warn me of what was happening, I felt they were, if anything, on the side of the robbers, so I ran right by them. As I did, one man called out, "Wha happen, man? Wha happen?" Without missing a step, I called out, "A whole heap of wrongs a gwaan in the club," and kept high-stepping it by them.

At Windward Road I had a decision to make. I could turn left, more quickly reaching a taxi stand but running in the same direction as the traffic. (Jamaicans drive on the left side of the road.) Right would take me on a long desolate stretch past the madhouse, but seemed safer from pursuit by car. I turned right. After running three blocks, I managed to flag down a taxi and convinced the driver to take me to the Rollington Town Police Station.

THE ROLLINGTON TOWN POLICE STATION

Not a police car was in sight, only unmarked cars. If there was a sign saying that this was a police station, I missed it. I asked the taxi man if he was sure this was a police station and he said, yes, go on in. Not a soul was in uniform. But a number of tall, dark, well-built men dressed in dark colors were standing around. The oldest stood behind a counter and I told him I had been robbed at the Village Club. He asked what they took. I told him and then unwisely continued, "But they missed my gold chain," and drawing back my shirt to show him, I was about to say, "And US$300 in my wallet," when he cut me off with a gruff voice. "Whaa? Dem leave you wid something?!" Rasta George, I thought to myself, after all these years you don't know better than to tell the police late at night in Jamaica that you still have something worth stealing?

When I told the man that the robbery was still going on he directed two men to drive me back to the club. Each was young but serious-looking, wearing dark slacks and a dark shirt. We got into a dark, unmarked car and sped at fifty and sixty miles an hour, with our lights out, through the mostly deserted and dark streets of East Kingston.

I RETURN WITH THE POLICE

When we arrived at the club, a crowd had gathered outside. The robbery was over and the thieves had gone in the other direction, over the back zinc fence. People were happy and excited and recounting the recent adventure. Almost immediately, a young woman came up to me and, in front of the police, said, "Bob! Me nebber know is you! I never recognize you in dat hat." Sure enough I was not wearing my customary, "Rasta tam," which is like a knitted sailor's cap, but was instead wearing a broader-rimmed hat I had recently bought in Panama. I naively thought at the time that it gave me a sophisticated, devil-may-care look. In fact, in the Rasta tam I at least looked conscious - or even like undercover police, as Huey Newton believed I was mistaken for in East Oakland after-hours clubs, to my own safety. But in the broad-rimmed hat and Filipino guayabara shirt, I looked like exactly what I was — an easy mark.

Then she said something I thought was truly astonishing. "Bob! If I'd known a you, I would never have let you go in there and get those wrongs!" My God, I thought, it's not wise to admit in front of the police to aiding and abetting a crime. But the police paid no attention. Then an old lady, short, dark, and grey-haired, came up and said to me, "Massah, me nebber know white man could fly, until I see you go by." She had apparently been in the crowd halfway down the road when I made my escape. The crowd erupted in laughter. A festive spirit settled on us all. We were happy to be alive. We now shared the joy of the experience, such as it was.

Finally, a policeman turned to me and said, "Doc! Doc, we don't think this is a safe neighborhood for you tonight." I was inclined to agree. They suggested they drive me to a taxi stand where I could catch a taxi to my hotel. We were soon underway, me in the back seat, when a remarkable conversation took place between the two officers in the front.

A SOCIALIST ROBBERY?

One cop turned to the next and said in patois (I believe perhaps with the assumption that I wouldn't understand or, more likely, would not do a thing if I did), "I don't care who approve this thing, I don't think is a good idea. I don't care if it was so-and-so at the community level or someone at the district level. It is not a good idea because you never know who you are going to buck up against!" His partner agreed. That must be me, I thought. Jamaica was very sensitive to any damage to foreigners. I was not, strictly speaking, a tourist, but I was a citizen of the United States, with a light skin, whose death in a botched, government-sanctioned robbery could exact disproportionate costs in the tourist trade. Everything else had gone according to plan. The Jamaican who was gun-butted, for example, was, I later learned, a regular at the club, coming every week or two with his ghetto blaster and several hundred dollars to spend. I was the fly in the ointment, making an unexpected appearance. My value to the larger community lay in my skin color and my nationality. Alive, I stood as a living symbol of tourism, an industry that at that time brought one visitor to the island every year per two residents. Dead, I represented a somewhat different image. So sensitive is the U.S. media to mishaps striking its citizens abroad, that even when the victims are only two Jamaicans guarding the U.S. Embassy their murders frighten Americans at home. If the U.S. Embassy itself was under attack, would Americans really be able to relax on the North Coast beaches? A raft of cancellations greeted the beginning of the tourist season, the murders having been timed to occur a few weeks earlier. But as an election device, if so it was intended, it failed: the PNP retained power in 1976.

In any case, the police appeared to be saying that the entire robbery was a community affair, approved by local politicians and sanctioned by the police themselves. This little socialist robbery, insofar as the authorities were involved, was an instance of revolutionary justice, an extra-judicial form of punishment sanctioned by the state. It was a concept that was popular in progressive circles in the 1970s. If the robbery really was an instance of state-sanctioned extra-judicial justice, I was more protected than I'd thought. Indeed, the next day I learned that as I made my move to the door, one robber called out, "See the white man there, him gone," and the leader said, "Let him go." I also learned that the owner had locked his safe and left the premises an hour before the robbery. Although one or two women were said to have been roughed up, I know of at least two who were in on the robbery, and I never saw any evidence the women were harmed. One man was gun butted, one shot in the neck (not fatally), the cook was hit on the head. Otherwise there were no physical injuries. Yet the take could not have been very high either. A thousand Jamaican dollars perhaps (US$200), or two thousand and some assorted property? Barely enough to pay the robbers themselves, much less a larger network. Two policemen, I understand, spent the night with two of the women to keep the premises safe and that, too, must be factored in somewhere as a cost or benefit.

That night at the Sheraton I had to ask for a new room. The robbers had my room key. The staff was amused by the reason for the change, but I was not. The hotel itself seemed mildly hostile under the socialists (PNP). The price of the room had risen while service and occupancy had plummeted. You were alone in the elevator and in the hallway. You could easily imagine a gang of robbers having the run of several stories of the hotel late at night. In the morning I reported to the police station, as requested, in order to fill out some forms. The cook was there as were a few other victims. The excitement of the robbery and our survival had now worn off. We were all a little depressed. That evening my brother-in-law drove me to the countryside but not before passing through some rough and dreaded roads in West Kingston. We turned down one narrow street to find it partly blocked by a motorcycle and three men working on it, none of whom showed the slightest interest in clearing a path. My brother-in-law, a stout and solidly built auto mechanic, started cursing and driving his car in little spurts at the offending roadblock. My God, I thought, I survived an armed robbery and the police, now I'm going to be killed in some street confrontation, possibly intentionally orchestrated, on a dark alley in West Kingston. But no, the men slowly cleared a path and my brother-in-law, cursing loudly the entire time, pushed his way through.

It was two days later in the countryside that I developed the illusion that a third of my head had been blown off, a sensation that lasted for nearly a week. This is something I have repeatedly noted. The actual event brings forth at the moment the kinds of reactions that may save your life – fight or flight, adrenaline – but once saved you experience the fright of how close you came to losing it all.

THE VILLAGE CLUB IN THE 1980S

For several years, strangely enough, I felt no desire to return to the Village Club. But in 1986 I met a young lady in Montego Bay who, it turned out, said she lived in what remained of the Village, so when next I was in Kingston I picked up a car mechanic friend who used to work with my brother-in-law in East Kingston and took him on a mission with me to the Club. My mechanic friend was a bit shorter than I but very powerfully built. About forty years of age, he had been trained in the British army in a series of killing and immobilizing maneuvers and had the additional advantage of being known in the area. Nevertheless, I felt tense and frightened as we drove up to the club. The road was pitted and the neighborhood looked poorer and more crowded than in the 1970s. The street, in turn, had crashed in on the club. The door and high front fence were gone, vehicles in various stages of disrepair were parked where I had been robbed, and three mechanics were at work. The front was now an auto-repair business. What lay behind it was anyone's guess.

CHAPTER 8

Glenroy Ramsey: Master Lizard Catcher

You run into uniquely talented people in all walks of life. One such person for me was Glenroy Ramsey, a school dropout whom I first hired to catch lizards for me when he was twelve. He was the greatest lizard-catcher I have ever met. This is saying something stronger than you might think because I have likely handled more Jamaican tree-climbing lizards than any human alive and have regularly employed youngsters ages twelve to sixteen to catch them for me. I have also caught lizards in Haiti, Panama, Cuba, East Africa, Europe, and the U.S. and I have never seen the likes of Mr. Ramsey. If there were an All-Jamaica Lizard-Catching Team that competed internationally (as do cricketers) Glenroy would certainly be on the team and would very likely be one of those rare individuals whose exploits are heralded for decades.

Let me give you two examples of Mr. Ramsey's special powers. Glenroy once caught the largest male green lizard I ever handled, and he also caught the largest female. This was not terribly surprising since he probably caught about one-third of all the green lizards I ever handled. What was truly exceptional was that he caught the two at the same moment, while they were copulating with each other, slipping a nylon noose of fishing-line around both their heads before jerking them off the tree in one sweet motion. To have the largest two lizards sexing with each other is such a statistically rare event as to constitute a valid scientific fact. In other words, in principle, as a scientist

I could have published a short note in a journal such as Herpetologica based almost entirely on this capture.

A second rare achievement suggests that the Lord Herself may have been intervening in Mr. Ramsey's exploits. Two scientists from Florida were visiting me at my work in Southfield, St. Elizabeth. They were studying crabs in bromeliads but wished to see the lizards I was studying, especially the green lizard and the coffee lizard. Too involved in conversation to go out myself with him, I asked Glenroy to capture a large male of either species. In less than fifteen minutes, he returned with a large male green lizard hanging by its neck from his noose. Protruding from the male's mouth were the hind feet and tail of another lizard. When we pulled this lizard out, it turned out to be a large male coffee lizard, dead for some time and enveloped in slime! Once again, Mr. Ramsey had performed way beyond ordinary expectation. This time he had caught two *species* at the same time. Incidentally, it was not beyond Glenroy to have concocted the entire exhibit himself, capturing each male separately and forcing one down the throat of the other. But this would have been very difficult to achieve and the direct physical evidence indicated otherwise: the male coffee lizard showed too many signs of having been inside the green lizard too long. It was, in fact, the green lizard's considerable difficulty swallowing his prey that permitted a relatively easy capture.

Glenroy and I often worked together as a team. When green lizards were frightened by our approach, they sometimes took to the very top leaves of their tree. Although Glenroy scaled the tree, he could not always sight the lizard himself (if it was flattened, for example, on top of a large mango leaf). When this happened, I usually directed the attack from the ground, watching through binoculars and giving instructions to help him maneuver his lizard stick close to the prey. Others would be helping us as well, giving Glenroy directions from their perches within the tree. When finally the noose slipped over the lizard's head, someone would yell, "Jig!" and Glenroy would sweep the lizard into the air. After this, I would measure the lizard, record its sex, and paint a number on the back for immediate recognition. This permitted us to study individuals in nature, and we also clipped two or three toes to give each lizard a permanent number since they shed their skin every three or four weeks and, along with it, our paint.

HE ONLY LOOKED FOR THEIR EYES

We once asked Glenroy what he looked for when he headed out to capture lizards. Most people look for the head jutting out from a branch or trunk. Sometimes we look for a tail or the general outline of a lizard. But Glenroy said he only looked, "For the eyes." We all had a good laugh at that one. After all, most of the lizards are small enough as it is without restricting our vision to their eyes alone! As the years rolled by, though, I came to see this as a very significant fact about Glenroy's approach. The sighting of eyes plays an extremely prominent role in predator-prey relations in nature. Even when prey play dead – play possum, for example – they invariably keep their eyes wide open. Eyes glisten with the consciousness and attentiveness of their possessors. Predators also key in on the eyes of their prey because a strike at the head will disable and kill. This bias led to the evolution of numerous eye-mimics: fake eyes located, for example, on the wings of butterflies so as to deflect the predator's attack onto a relatively dispensable part of the anatomy.

Perhaps Glenroy had a special ability to concentrate on the eyes and this accounts, in small part, for his outsize skill at catching lizards. That is one possibility but who knows how the interaction actually works? For all we know, some lizards seeing Glenroy coming their way say to themselves (so to speak), "Rasta George! I can't look this devil in the eye, he'd recognize me! I'd better get the hell out of here," thus making a movement and attracting the attention of the eyes it is seeking to avoid.

By the way, I said "in some small part" above because you should not imagine for a moment that Glenroy's skill was just a matter of some eye trick or trick with lizard eyes. To appreciate the brainpower behind his success you had to watch him mature as a tactician to take on the most difficult challenges. In our later years together a capture might go as follows: upon sighting a lizard he would see at a glance that this was going to be a difficult capture: the lizard was a small adult female, already nervous at our presence, in a tree with too much canopy and too many escape routes. He would then devise a strategy, closing off escape routes, positioning others to watch from key angles, maneuvering the lizard through his own climbing approach and stick movements. Some epic struggles between man and lizard lasted half an hour

TWO BIGGEST LIZARDS SEXING. Within a more recent smaller study area, it seems that the largest male prefers the largest female and vice-versa. (Photo courtesy Robert Trivers.)

or longer, and when Glenroy finally emerged from the tree with lizard in hand, the lizard knew that it had been had, that it had run up against a superior force, been worn down by a greater mind. Of course, Glenroy used other minds than his own in his campaign, and the entire operation was bankrolled by Harvard University, not to mention the United States government, but it was Glenroy's great skill that tamed almost all of the difficult lizards, leaving only the occasional female to run and hide from the Greater Southfield Cooperative Lizard Catching Team, permanently postponing her encounter with science.

That his various abilities have a genetic component seems very likely. His grandfather was a legendary praedial larcenist. Here is one famous trick of his. He would not steal your cow, but would rather walk on all fours toward her at three in the morning, with tall grass stems tied to every part of his body. This served as camouflage from the owner and food for the cow. While he milked her, she ate the grass he'd kindly provided. After that, she always looked forward to his return and would not greet him with any unpleasant sounds that might attract human attention.

The lizards had less to fear from us than they supposed. We rarely killed a lizard through rough capture. The lizard would lose two toenails, to be sure, but so would everyone else in the study area, so no particular injustice was implied. (We never cut their large toe on the hind leg out of respect for its obvious utility.) But the lizards never grew to love us, that is certain, and later recaptures only made matters worse. It eventually became apparent that the lizards could tell us from other people in the area. For some time I imagined this might be due to my light skin color, an easy cue, but one day I learned that this was certainly not a necessary one. I was hidden behind a bush watching a large, male green lizard from a great distance through binoculars. The lizard was perched, bright green, on a mango trunk about fifteen feet off the ground, faced down. Jamaican after Jamaican walked by in both directions, some passing quite close without any obvious response from the lizard. Suddenly the giant green lizard took one quick look up the street, turned and bolted for the foliage above. I looked up the street and saw two of my lizard catchers with bun and box juice in hand returning from the shop. Neither carried a stick (another obvious cue) but both had heads tilted slightly back and, through long habit, frequently raked the trees with their eyes. Perhaps this was the lizard's cue or perhaps by now he knew the odious sight of each and every one of us, regardless of the way in which we approached!

LETTING GANJA OPEN UP YOUR EYES

One day while we were hunting green lizards, a large male on a very tall tree took off running to the top the minute he saw us. The tree had a long bare trunk with only a small cluster of vegetation halfway up and then a decent clump at the top. My thirteen-to fourteen-year-old workers faced a sixty-foot climb, but before beginning they promptly sat down and rolled three big-head spliffs. I looked on with dismay as they smoked their ganja. The tree looked terrifying to me, even in my current sober state, and I could not imagine anyone safely navigating it with a good load of ganja under his belt. I saw it all in a flash: one would lose his grip and plummet forty feet to a horrible death. I would have a mangled youngster's body to rush directly to Black River Hospital. Dead on Arrival. I would be a pariah in the community and feel a deep guilt for the rest of my life.

In addition, word of the calamity would certainly reach Harvard where the matter would be investigated and it would turn out that I had not only condoned the climb itself but massive infusions of ganja before the climb. This would make it very unlikely that the University would wish to continue any kind of relationship with me. So everything was on the line. Ten minutes later they clamored down the tree, green lizard dangling from a noose. I said a silent prayer of thanks and asked them why on earth they smoked the ganja before they caught the lizard. Why not afterwards? "Because the ganja opens our eyes," they sang out. Probably so, but it sure scared the hell out of me.

One day I was measuring a lizard when Glenroy and two of his assistants appeared, all bright-eyed and asked, "Rasta, how much would you pay to see two *humans* sex?" I had to laugh. I had been paying them a full day's adult wages working in someone's field (US$2) to show me two lizards having sex – surely it would break the bank to show me two humans! And the copulation was in my study area, in an abandoned tailor shop – I could in principle open a parallel study into human copulations! But I declined – even when they offered to show it to me for free.

GLENROY ATTACKS THE VERY FOUNDATION OF SCIENCE

Glenroy, as I learned in my later work, did not always catch the lizards where he was supposed to. That is, within the seven-acre study site. This problem didn't arise during the first year and, later, it never happened during the first two or three weeks we were at the site. Un-captured lizards were plentiful then and there was no need to violate rules. But as most of the lizards were captured and painted, fewer and fewer unmarked ones remained to catch, yet the need to concentrate on these was greater, since each incremental increase in the percentage of lizards caught improved the quality of my data in all directions – estimates of survival, growth, copulatory success, and so on. Consequently I increased the pay rate, but this only increased the temptation to bring in outside lizards.

At first, I believe, Glenroy simply hunted immediately outside the study area whenever my attention was preoccupied, measuring and marking lizards that had just been caught. When I was not preoccupied we travelled as a group. But as time wore on he started specializing in this deceit. I learned that early in the morning on his way to my study site he sometimes picked up two or three lizards – usually large, dumb males, easy to catch. He kept them in empty cardboard juice containers, secreted them on my study site, and habitually went to this cache when I was busy elsewhere, and "caught" me a new lizard. He was, in fact, catching lizards inside my study site, but, alas, they were imported lizards.

I became dimly aware that something was amiss when late in a visit, while I was preoccupied marking females, Glenroy started appearing with large, unmarked males. But I didn't fully catch on until one day I came across a male in the afternoon a third of a kilometer toward the opposite end of my study site from where I vividly remembered marking him that morning. For one wild moment I imagined that there was a small category of super-males that traveled, "like a rolling stone, gathering no moss" and impregnating females all along their path. But, no, nothing so exciting. This male was trying to return home; he had been captured very early in the morning down the road by Glenroy and transported to my study site; he was now moving rapidly in the reverse direction – that is, toward home.

Later, as a good pretend-scientist, I did an analysis of the data to see whether the patterns tended to look different later in my studies than earlier - that is, whether Glenroy's trick was actually changing the results in a way that showed up in the data. The patterns did not vary over the course of studies, so I left the matter where it was. I did not refer to the problem in my thesis.

SELF–DECEPTION NEARLY TAKES US OVER A CLIFF

I nearly killed Glenroy and myself on a trip we took up into the Blue Mountains to catch the elusive "water lizard," who can only be found at about twelve hundred meters above sea level. And I would have killed the driver in the bargain, as well as a young woman from Clarendon who was along for what she imagined would be a fun ride in the mountains. What she got instead was a near-death experience.

The problem was that she was *my* date, and she had been showing undue attraction to the young driver who was then about twenty-six. He was muscular, dark-skinned, and he drove the car skillfully, every turn controlled in his gut, his broad shoulders whipping from side to side the better to control the small steering wheel attached to our large black Capri automobile. Such an arrangement was, indeed, called a "muscle car," since it required considerable muscle to turn the large car on a small wheel. From the back seat, my forty-three-year-old eyes shone with jealousy, as they watched her admiration for the driver climb with every hundred meters of altitude skillfully negotiated. I saw only his growing stature in her eyes, not the growing danger of a misstep at the altitudes he had already achieved. Naïvely I imagined that a simple replacement of me for him would restore the status quo ante, her eyes glazing over in admiration as *my* body now controlled the Capri for general benefit. As I say, I gave scant attention to the fact that this little psychodrama was not being acted out at ground level but instead at about eight hundred meters above it, with hundred meter plunges revealing themselves just meters to one's left as one fought to control an overly large car with an unusually small steering wheel and, of course, traveling faster than warranted even under optimal conditions.

In any case, such was soon the case, the driver now safe in back, me at the helm when our car struck some gravel on the far side of the road, which temporarily pulled us toward the precipice – temporarily, that is, if the previous driver had still been in control, for he would have jerked the car back on track. Instead, my weaker, slower response failed to do the trick and we drifted toward a precipice, there opening up a plunge so deep one couldn't see the bottom, only a tree some six meters down, which just might catch or slow our fall on the way to certain doom below. But a sandy ridge at the very left-hand side of the road stopped our slide, catching our undercarriage as we tilted, three wheels in the air. The woman screamed. I scrambled out of the car first and had to reach down and pull out the young woman, the car tilting downward toward her window. Out came the driver and Glenroy from the back window. We were all humbled by our near catastrophe and very happy to be alive. We even poured a little white rum – and threw several ganja seeds – over the edge in humble thanks to a merciful Jahovia-dread.

No sooner done, than a truckload of soldiers careened around the corner, going downhill, and twenty men jumped out to admire how close we had come to death without actually dying. As if in unison ten or twelve grabbed the car and heaved it back on the road. Not even a flat tire and not a scratch on any of us. One big, bright-looking man peered in the driver's window and said, "Ahh, I see the problem. Your steering is too small. See this big car wants a bigger steering wheel." He called the others over and everyone agreed. Yes, indeed, I admitted, this steering wheel is too damn small. But my main activity was sopping my brow with the remaining white rum, the better to cool down the overheated brain that – far more than the steering wheel – had brought us so close to death.

This little matter of forgetting that you are eight hundred meters up, I believe, is a major reason I have been frightened of heights ever since I was a child. To forget a simple fact like that you are more than two meters above ground level may be charming and, indeed, revolutionary where theory is concerned, but in real life it can be fatal. Small wonder that whenever I am forced into a tree above my head, I consciously try to enervate each of my limbs separately, so as to require four independent acts of forgetting before I plummet to the ground. I do not think Ernst Mayr, the great evolutionary biologist, is as absent-minding as I am, but he certainly possesses intense powers of concentration and this may help explain his own great fear of heights.

GLENROY CATCHES A CROCODILE BY HAND

In later years, I saw Glenroy, or Rammy as he was called, in Alligator Pond

THE CLIFF. This is the spot, or close to it, where I almost took our car over the cliff. The sand to the left caught us. Kingston is well below. (Photo courtesy Adam Wilson.)

where he lived. He was an expert diver and swimmer. He once captured a small crocodile – alive, by hand – a feat that sufficiently amazed the fishing community of Alligator Pond so as to attract a crowd of admirers all day long, earning Rammy $600 Jamaican in photo commissions from tourists. Two policemen investigated the capture without molesting Glenroy in the slightest, even though capturing crocodiles was illegal. More remarkably, they didn't molest the crocodile; often a captured crocodile is shot on sight by the police as a menace to humans.

Even small crocs are dangerous. The one-meter croc Glenroy caught (not counting the tail) could have taken off his hand or, at least, left it badly mangled. Not only are the crocodile's famous jaws formidable, the powerful thrashing tail is lined on both sides with long rows of razor sharp, half-inch blades. Struggling with this creature in your arms might leave you with a very unpleasant set of half-inch razor blade slices crisscrossing most of your body.

As related by Rammy, the capture took place as follows. He was taking an early morning swim in the cool Alligator River (what biologists would call a "crocodile," Jamaicans call an "alligator") and when he surfaced from a dive he noticed at eye level – about twenty meters across the river – a crocodile asleep on his favorite morning basking place, a mangrove branch a half meter above the water. Glenroy was used to seeing the croc basking at this spot to warm up early each morning. Usually the croc was alert and, once it spotted Rammy at a distance of twenty meters, it would begin to flee, slipping into the water and swimming away. This time, though, the croc was asleep.

Glenroy did not pause two seconds before deciding to catch the crocodile by hand. The local hotel had a standing offer to buy any living crocodile brought to them. Their previous one, used for display – to entice prospective visitors – had recently escaped. It was beautiful to watch Glenroy tell the story, especially the first time. He had circled in the water and emerged some twenty meters distant to creep quietly into the mangroves growing from the land. The twenty meters he had traversed in a tight, coiled pattern, his whole mind intent on soundlessness, the large reptile being very sensitive to any unusual sound and quick to respond. When Glenroy mimicked standing over the animal, his shoulder and arms began to expand, his face took on a dreadful predatory snarl, his whole frame tensed, especially his gut. He bent over, and suddenly his two poised arms leapt out like twin snakes and grabbed both the head and the base of the tail in one fierce movement.

The crocodile awoke to find himself being lifted off his perch. One hand was wrapped tightly around his jaw, just in front of the eyes. A second hand (Glenroy's stronger, right hand) was gripping the base of his thick and powerful tail. The croc attempted to throw his body into violent convulsions, but Glenroy met every twist with a counter twist, his whole body tight, stomach muscles straining. Concentrating on keeping the croc in a straight line, he carried him toward the beach.

RAMMY AND ME. Glenroy leaning against me at Alligator Pond near his shop. (Trivers File Photo.)

WHAT TO DO WHEN A CROCODILE COMES STRAIGHT AT YOU?

Someone asked Glenroy what he would do if a large crocodile were headed straight toward him at the surface of the water. You can bet we all leaned forward to hear his answer. After all, any of us might end up in this situation, and Glenroy's advice promised to replace blind panic with a sensible plan. As it so often is, the ideal plan turned out to be counterintuitive. Glenroy said he would face the crocodile, swim *toward* it, and then at the last moment dive deeply underneath it. The crocodile's problem, Glenroy explained, is that it has a very stiff backbone. It has tremendous strength in its tail and can propel itself rapidly on the surface or in a dive, but it has a very limited maneuverability and can turn only a few degrees at a time. Thus, the croc would not be able to dive after you, somersaulting so as to chase you immediately from behind. Sideways turning would take quite some time, during which it would be swept further in the direction of its forward movement, giving you even more time to reach safety after surfacing.

And what if the crocodile dove as it approached you? Your response would depend on how far away it was. If only twenty meters, you would still swim toward the croc, but now stay right at the surface and rapidly pass *over* it. Here, Glenroy made some loud, splashing kind of swimming motions at the surface. You were at no time trying to hide from the croc, just to get out of its way in a manner that would leave it a hard task if it meant to pursue you.

The good news was, it rarely wanted to. In fact, the croc's limited mobility is what makes it so unfortunate to run into one of these creatures in the first place. Imagine you are swimming upstream and a crocodile is moving at a good clip straight towards you. Its response to anything in its way is to open its mouth and keep coming. It may be able to steer around an object but it still does not wish to create new steering problems for itself further downstream. The problem, Glenroy said, is that, "You're in his way!" Here a little bit of righteous anger crept into Glenroy's voice, so animated was he in discussing life from the crocodile's viewpoint. There is a natural traffic along the river's flow and you are not abiding by it. Glenroy explained that he watched very carefully the direction of movement of any croc coming toward him and simply swam so as to increase the distance at which they passed. He showed how in some cases a croc must take a unique path to its underwater hole, certain approaches being foreclosed by its inability to make sharp turns. Every croc has its own river hole, he explained, and it is best for your safety to find out where it is.

Rammy's croc stories reminded me of the legendary Phil Darlington, Curator of Beetles at the Museum when I was a graduate student and the master of zoogeography, the distribution of animal species over time and space. We feared him because he was a tall, lanky, dour, elderly character who did not invite easy banter. But there was one reason we all loved him. He had a pronounced limp on one side and he'd gained this, we were told, in the service of evolutionary biology. As the story went, he was walking along a rope ladder above a river in Indonesia when a crocodile leapt up and grabbed his leg, and hauled him into the river. A croc likes to pull you under water, whip you around and drown you. On his way down, Darlington was alleged to have said to himself in righteous anger, "Wait a second, you don't collect *us* as specimens, *we* collect *you*!" In any case, he managed to free himself and reach safety, and he'd gained the limp that earned our affection in the bargain.

Glenroy and I have remained life-long friends. I visit him now and again at his little shack where the Alligator River empties into the ocean. He sells drinks and, if the season is right, fried fish. It's the river that attracts crocodiles since they seek out freshwater habitats in which to breed. The other day he came up to Southfield and spent the day spotting green lizards for me. All he had to do was wander around or indeed stand still, and he would spot lizard after lizard, especially the females and small immature males, which are more difficult to spot. He was never as skilled at deception as he was at detection, and perhaps that's not a coincidence. But that hasn't been an issue between us for many years – nothing left to fool me about. We plan to take a trip shortly into the Blue Mountains in search of the elusive "water lizard."

I had just written the above when I learned that Rammy was a patient at the Mandeville Hospital, having been attacked at four a.m. on the way home from a wake by a man alleging that Glenroy had been stealing his firewood.

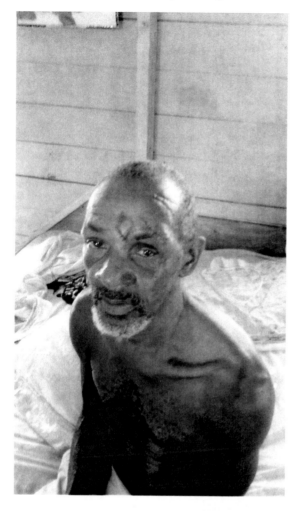

RAMMY AFTER ATTACK. Rammy recovering after a surprise machete attack on him. (Photo courtesy Dayemeon Edwards.)

Ramsey lay in the road for a half hour after the attack before passersby rescued him. No bones were broken but there were numerous lacerations requiring stitches; he awaits an operation to see if they can save his left eye.

CHAPTER 9

Jamaican Murders
Most Frequent
and Most Foul

It used to be said some forty years ago in Jamaica that if you wanted to murder someone, you should bring him first to Southfield because no one has ever been convicted of murder in Southfield. I am not sure if this still holds true, but nor do I know of a single counter-example. And I do know of many murders committed in or nearby Southfield that met with no official punishment. My closest friend was murdered there. So was a good shopkeeper friend. I have almost been killed in an armed home invasion robbery as well as in a set-up at a bar. That is how prevalent murder (or attempted murder) is in Jamaica at the local level alone.

Murders, of course, are not trivial evolutionary events. At least one person is dead and another responsible. There must be a deeper evolutionary logic to account for a society where murder is so prevalent, but I don't know what it is beyond such simple arguments that the evidence decomposes much more rapidly in the tropics, on multiple fronts, than in the temperate zone. A corpse, for example – minus the bones and dentition – will decompose overnight in the tropics while surviving intact for months, years, and even hundreds of years in the arctic.

THE LINK

A typical murder in the old days might run as follows. Someone is at your window at two thirty in the morning. Aunt Elsie is having convulsions, can you come drive her to hospital? You get dressed, you step outside, you are promptly shot to death. The key man is the one at the window. It's always someone known to you. The murderers are a gang from Kingston, bent on robbery (their pay in the enterprise) or straight-out paid work as assassins. They are whisked quickly out of the community, so only the local link is available. Nothing is known about the Kingston crew. Rumors swirl, but nothing happens.

In the old days (thirty or forty years ago), transportation to Kingston was via 'minibuses' seating a maximum of twenty with a driver and a side-man. The side-man opened the side door, collected fares and helped pack in as many passengers as humanly possible. He was the dangerous man on the bus because he could so easily act as the key link. You get on your usual mini-bus in rural Southfield at 6:40 in the morning, expecting to reach Kingston, after many stops, by 8:30. At May Pen, two robbers enter the bus, one with a gun. They proceed to rob the bus but when they come to you, they start yelling as if you are not cooperating, put two slugs in you, and hurriedly finish off the robbery. Story is told as a botched robbery resulting in the unnecessary death of one of the passengers. But in fact it is an assassination, the side-man being the key since he is the link to the victim and the gang. As they come onto his bus, he covertly fingers the victim, whom they finish off before quickly ending the robbery and departing. Who feh know, who feh say?

Another example in the genre occurred as follows. A link once brought a gang from Kingston to rob a money-changer in Southfield, because he was assumed to have large sums of money at home ready to be changed into the appropriate currency (Jamaican to U.S.). The link was both the key and a direct beneficiary, but the father of the money-changer realized at the last moment what was going on and blocked the door with his foot. The link promptly shot through the door, thereby gaining entrance, but at the cost of killing the old man. The money-changer high-charged it out the back, carrying whatever money he had, if he had any to begin with. These facts were known to everyone, including the police. Another unresolved Jamaican murder.

A VERY BITTER MURDER

Joe was an outsider in the community, having arrived some six years before from the neighboring parish of Westmoreland. He had come courting Ms. SP, whom he married and with whom he had two children. He worked as a porter at the Black River Hospital. He was very well liked – handsome, friendly, calm, and quiet. He fit in with everyone. I hardly knew him, but one night at Celestine's bar he said he wanted to talk to me in private, perhaps at another bar. He suggested we have some drinks together. He was already drinking a stiff glass of rum, but I hardly drank, being then strictly a ganja man. I didn't want to drink at a bar and I invited him up to my library, which I was in the process of dismantling so I could take it with me to Panama, where I would spend the coming year and to which I was flying in several days.

He came the next day and, sad to say, I have very little memory of what he wished to talk about. I know I was distracted by my library work as we sat together. He hinted at problems in his life, and I got the impression that he wanted to share them with me because we were both outsiders – married into the area but not born there. He didn't make his concerns more precise and, to my shame, I never pressed him to share with me what was troubling him.

To my shame, I say, because two weeks later Joe lay dead, his body found in a field, a container of poison nearby and his mouth reeking of it – he had apparently committed suicide by drinking the poison. All of this I heard from my wife who was still in Southfield and who called me with the news. When I returned, I learned other details. His body looked as if it had been laid down to rest on the grass where it was found. There was no evidence of struggle, of convulsions, of him having moved about – no bent, torn, or shredded grass. Nothing. This was all the more surprising because the poison was not the quick-acting version that caused death at once, but a slower-acting poison that took about an hour to kill its victim, plenty of time to move about and thrash around. There were also signs of trauma to his head and upper body.

Turned out, he had had an argument with his wife, who had called her brother who had called a friend, a notorious punk who fashioned himself a real Jamaican "bad man." Together they are said to have attacked Joe in his home so as to render him unconscious and then strangled him – the death scene arranged to provide an alternative scenario of suicide by poison. I'm sure the police never checked to see if there was any appreciable amount of poison in Joe

Oh, how I grieved his dirty murder! I doubt I could have done much, on the way off the island as I was, but had I known what he was afraid of I certainly could have spoken unambiguously to his dear wife, warning her of what I would do if she went ahead with her plans to harm him.

From what I understand, the police were not so stupid as to miss an obvious set-up. The murderers had a brother-in-law who ran a large car-repair enterprise nearby and who was said to have "bought out the case." This is common in Jamaica. "There is no justice in Jamaica," is a common expression and buying out is a large part of the reason why. Any case can be bought out. The expense depends on both the seriousness of the crime and on any beneficent political connections one might have.

POLICE MURDERS

Police murders are so common in Jamaica as to be part of the fabric of daily life. They take a variety of forms, executions in the line of duty being one of the most common. Forty years ago it was said that every evening police in Kingston were issued two "picks" of herb and a ratchet knife (something like a switch-blade) so as to plant them on anyone they chose to shoot dead. Since the prison term then for being found with a "pick" was eighteen months in prison at hard labor, it was just barely plausible that a poor man might go up against armed police officers with only a ratchet knife in order to try to avoid a hellish eighteen months for nothing at all.

Here is a recent police killing. On July 7, 2012, a heart-rending photo in a local newspaper of a man weeping for his seventeen-year-old son, killed in a police "shoot out." His son, along with three young men in their twenties were killed during a police "operation" in his area. Police, as usual, claim the men fired at the police, while trying to outrun them, while the police were merely trying to apprehend wanted men. Residents said three of the men were returning from a dance in a car while the police lay in wait to ambush them. The seventeen-year-old was shot dead in his own home after the police kicked the door down. Police claimed an officer was shot, but this seems unlikely since nothing more was heard about him, nor the killing of the youths.

Or take this example. You make sense of it for me. A woman in her forties is returning home from a "nigh, nigh" (something like a wake) at twelve-thirty at night. She enters her yard, itself surrounded by a zinc fence. Fifty-two bullets are then fired through the zinc by a police patrol conducting "operations" in the area, killing the woman. Police claimed a shoot-out, but film showed only entry wounds in the zinc and no neighbor supported the police account. Of course there was an outcry, high-up officials visited, and nothing whatsoever was or will be done. In March 2014, there were 27 such killings of citizens in Kingston alone. In 2013 there were 258 police killings of Jamaican citizens.

Some police murders are pre-meditated assassinations. It is an open secret that death squads are maintained within the police under both political parties. Sometimes it is alleged that they are benign: known rapists and murderers that the "judicial" system is unable to convict are then handled "extra-judicially." A common method in Kingston is to roust a man from his bed in his underwear at three a.m. in West Kingston and then carry him to Rollington Town in East Kingston, shoot him, and leave him "a roadside." It will be reported in the newspapers as a bullet-riddled body of an unknown man in his underwear found on a Rollington Town road at six a.m. after inhabitants heard loud noises earlier in the morning. Is he actually a rapist or a murderer, is he someone whose death has been paid for to the police ahead of time, is he, maybe, of the wrong party at the wrong place, namely in his own bed? Or is he merely someone against whom a policeman has a private grudge? Who feh know? Who feh say? A dead him dead same way.

The most famous case of extra-judicial murder was the "Green Bay Massacre" – an example of "socialist justice" so incompetent that it actually unraveled almost immediately, attracting public notice sufficient to cause an investigation, so that we actually now know most of the story, though it is still widely denied by those politically affiliated with the guilty party.

THE GREEN BAY MASSACRE

This famous murder took place on January 5, 1978. About a dozen young supporters of the then-opposition Jamaican Labour Party were lured into a trap set by the Military Intelligence Unit within the Defense force, itself in charge of "covert operations." The Military Intelligence Unit was tasked with taking "all reasonable steps" to ensure removal of anyone considered a threat to national security or the smooth running of their government. That is, their mandate was an explicit policy of assassination based on "threat."

The youths all came from a heavily labor district in Kingston, Southside, and were members of a gang called the "POW Posse," which was believed to be too closely associated with the opposition party. The posse was duly infiltrated, and fourteen individuals were identified for elimination. These were all offered guns and work and invited to come to what was an army shooting range in Green Bay, St Catherine. There they assembled, and a short time later a pistol shot sounded out. This was the signal to surrounding soldiers to unleash a torrent of rifle fire on the unsuspecting boys. With typical socialist incompetence they were only able to kill five. The rest fled into the bush. One was rescued by fishermen in a nearby river. Thus did we learn what socialist justice looked like. The socialists argued that it was a morally justified operation since by agreeing to guns and other free goods, the youths had revealed their strong counter-revolutionary bent.

Huey Newton, by the way, was openly derisive of this operation, which he did not consider true socialist justice. The problem, in his view, was that the boys had not done a single thing wrong; they were prepared to receive the tools of their trade but had done nothing more than agree to this free gift.

By contrast Huey told me what socialist justice looked like when dispensed properly. A Black Panther Party member who lived in a first floor apartment in a building owned by the Party was raped one night by a strong young neighbor, who crawled in through a window to do his deed. The penalty for rape in the Party was death, whether it was done by someone within the party or performed by an outsider. Huey immediately moved the woman out of the apartment and into a new one, where she received mail while he arranged for mail in someone's new name to arrive at the empty apartment. Then, after six weeks, she moved back in, shades open, available. Sure enough, that night the rapist crawled through the window again, only this time a second party member was waiting, gun in hand. The man was shot on the way in: he had tried, convicted, and executed himself in one act.

There were multiple investigations of the Green Bay massacre. No one was found guilty of anything. No one was even accused. One jury ruled that the soldiers were guiltless because they had fired in self-defense out of fear that their unarmed targets would shoot them first. When you are defending a bad hand, it is astonishing what you will claim makes sense.

"MY TIME COME!"

I knew Nikkie first as a young lad in the neighborhood. He occasionally caught lizards for me, but I mostly knew him through other connections. He was very bright and friendly and extremely strong. When he was seventeen years old he worked for me for three months building my house in Southfield. He was the second youngest and the strongest in a party of twelve men. When he and the second strongest man pushed a huge boulder uphill to form one corner of the house's foundation, Nikkie actually growled like a dog to give him the final strength to do it and we all enjoyed a good laugh. Nikkie once extracted a large rock out of the limestone after two others had failed, rolling it up the sides so skillfully that people burst out saying, "We have a tracti-vator, we have a tracti-vactor!" – that is, a tractor joined to an elevator.

Yet Nikkie came within an inch of losing his life twenty years later, caught up in some murder scheme whose meaning remains obscure to this day. In the summer of 2012, Nikkie lived in Mandeville and worked as the watchman over a wealthy woman's property. This woman was from Bermuda but was married to a Jamaican. Nikkie had driven to the airport to pick up his employer for her six-week visit to Jamaica and had hired his closest childhood friend to do the taxi work.

Upon arrival at the house, Nikkie carried some of his boss's bags into her home and had just returned to get the rest, when two gunmen appeared. One held a weapon to the cab driver's head, and the other directed his weapon at Nikkie's. It looked like a classic Jamaican robbery. It's not unusual for armed robbers to show up when you are known to be returning from the airport and so likely to be carrying money, jewelry, and other valuables.

Nikkie and his friend were herded into the boss's bedroom where she stood with her belongings facing the bed. Nikkie and his friend were ordered facedown on the floor while his boss was executed with two shots to her back. It was clear now that this was no robbery, but an assassination made to look like one. It's a convenient set-up: you can predict the arrival of the victim pretty precisely, and you can make the killing look like part of a robbery.

The killer moved past Nikkie and shot his taxi friend twice in the head. "Kill the other," he commanded his friend and left. Since he was using a snub-nosed 38, it had only five bullets and he was probably saving the last as personal insurance.

As Nikkie heard the command, he said to himself, "My time come: a dead, me a dead," but the man had a 9mm, which jammed. Nikkie heard a click. When he heard a second click, he said to himself, "My time DON'T come" and jumped up and hit the man hard enough on his lower neck that he wheeled back and dropped the gun. Nikkie picked it up, drew it back and forth – chuck-chuck – so as to un-jam the 9mm and fired after the fleeing gunman. In fact, he emptied his gun in a wild exhibition of shooting, firing off all nine shots, hitting no one. I had to say to him later, "You didn't want to reserve a couple of shots to protect yourself?" But he was in a panic and wanted to frighten off his attackers. In an assassination all witnesses are supposed to be eliminated.

Nikkie aroused a neighbor who was a doctor. The doctor called the police and Nikkie then called the Jamaican husband of the executed woman. Nikkie heard nothing like a shocked or pained reaction, more like, "Really? A dead, she really dead?" In any case, the Jamaican police promptly held Nikkie captive for two weeks on the grounds that since he alone survived the killing, he must have been in on the operation, perhaps the key link. During eighteen hours of questioning, they never asked him how the husband had responded to the bad news. At this point, he asserted his right to a lawyer and was placed in a cell full of real and alleged killers, often talking the night through on this or that murder they had actually committed (or claimed to have). I later asked him if he was ever attacked and he said no but that he had had to "muscle up" a couple of times. He did not eat during the entire incarceration and claims not to have slept either, though of course he must have – fitful, cautious and sporadic perhaps, but he certainly slept and likely dreamed. No one has ever been arrested for the crime.

THE NIGHT PETER TOSH DIED

I only met one of the legendary Wailers and it was Peter Tosh. I smoked a spliff with him at Harvard in 1975. It happened like this: I was an Associate Professor in Biology, and with my beautiful Jamaican wife in the audience of his concert at Harvard's Sanders Theater during his "Legalize It" tour. This was back when we were so naïve we actually believed legalization was just around the corner. Peter, as always pushing the envelope, began the U.S. tour by throwing marijuana joints into the audience until the police told him that technically speaking this was not yet legal. After that, he began his shows by throwing out rolling papers alone. Then the lights went out and a thousand points of light appeared.

I was so deluded that I imagined that Peter Tosh might be short of herb during his visit to Cambridge, so I rolled a giant "cock-head spliff" as a gift for him. At the intermission I walked up to a stagehand and gave him the spliff for Peter. The stagehand called Peter over and told him, "The man give you this." Peter looked at me and said, "Well, then let we burn it," so we stood in the Rasta circle and passed it on the heart's (left-hand) side. I smoked a spliff with the second most talented reggae artist in the world, short only of the legendary Bob Marley.

I never saw Peter again. But I did happen to be in Kingston on October 17, 1988, the night he was murdered. I had driven in from lizard work in the countryside to join a medical student friend at the University of the West Indies who knew some clubs in East Kingston that I did not and who was going to show them to me. These were not go-go but regular bars, frequented by both sexes. I was most eager to join him. I was due at his apartment on campus at 8:45 p.m.

I lay down at my hotel at 6:00 p.m. for my one-hour nap and promptly passed out for three full hours. This was before the use of cell phones in Jamaica, and by the time I reached his yard he was gone. The first thing I heard was his mother rushing out to ask, "You hear dem kill Peter? You hear dem kill Peter Tosh?" "A whaa yuaa tell me say? Peter Tosh?" She told me it had just come over the radio. Jesus F... Christ I thought, this evening is done, I miss my chance to visit a new set of clubs with a trusted friend and the immortal Peter Tosh, my smoking companion (or "I-dren") from Harvard days lies dead in nearby Barbicon. Any festive spirit was sucked out of me in one breath.

I retired to the nearest "go-go" club – or "nastiness club" as my mother-in-law called them – places where young girls danced on stage without much clothing and sometimes performed additional tricks out back. On the way in, I stopped to chat with "Jerkers." This was the man who did a little business barbecuing chicken ("jerking") on a grill fashioned out of halves of an oil drum. We were old friends because I smoked my little bit of weed with him, went in and watched some dancing, perhaps bought a drink or two, and then returned to smoking and chatting with him out front.

We were commiserating the passing of our dearly beloved Peter when a most extraordinary event occurred. A long fancy black limousine arrived and six dark-skinned, serious-looking men exited, all in tuxedos. "Rasta George, a de Mafia dis!" I said to myself. But then I noticed that the two men exiting from the rear each had a sub-machine gun pointed at the ground. "Rasta, a de Mafia INSIDE the police dis!" (since no ordinary criminals would carry their weapons in full view). Why on earth would dressed-up police be arriving at our humble club instead of scouring Kingston for the murderers of the then-greatest living Rasta artist?

"You don't know who they are?" asked Jerkers. "That is the owner of the club, that the dread officer who calls himself T, and all the other men are police." The men went into the Club. I waited a decent five minutes and followed them in. None of them were in sight. I asked the bartender if she had seen six men in tuxedos. Yes, she had. And where had they gone? Through this back door, indicating a door behind her. Am I allowed to go there? Yes, if you pay US$5. I paid and entered a large backyard I never knew existed and saw that the men were over in the girls' compound, a two-floor wooden structure in which each young woman had her own room, separate from any rooms reserved for commercial transactions. I was relatively fearless in those days and walked right over to see what was going on.

T stood at the top of the stairs with a modest "big man belly." Most of the officers were seated, and some had naked or near-naked girls sitting on their legs, while one of the men was absentmindedly diddling the girl on his leg. I took this scene in for a moment or so and then rejoined my friend Jerkers outside. What I had seen struck me as extraordinary. Why weren't these police officers driving all over Kingston looking for the murderers? Why were they instead at a go-go club acting for all the world like men who had just come from a job and wanted a little enjoyment, a little extra pay? Why the big difference between their high-class dress and their low-class environment? Shooting three people dead and shattering a woman's jawbone (part of the damage done to those in Peter's home) seems unlikely to be a sexual turn-on and, indeed, these men did not appear to be on a sexual high. They looked like they had come from some serious work and were in need of a diversion. But who, of course, am I to say, merely a curious on-looker? Hard set of men to turn away at your gate though, all dressed up in tuxedos, just dropping by for a friendly, high-class social visit.

Peter had a long, hostile relationship with the police, and was repeatedly locked up and once almost beaten to death with police truncheons for trivial offenses. He preached against the police in song and word, and was acerbic in style – Kingston was "Kill-some" – so there was no love lost there. He was also the only Wailer still performing, and his music was getting more rhythmic and subtle and his words more caustic. Just the person to create the post-Marley new beat that would threaten Bob's "dead left," as inheritance is

<small>PETER TOSH.</small> In 1974 during his *Legalize It* tour. (File Photo.)

called in Jamaica. I later heard a tape of his latest music, never to be released, and it was new and powerful.

Certainly the police were not expected to be his top supporters, and inside jobs have inherent advantages over outside ones. Since when do the police investigate themselves? Very rarely in my own country, and the more money on the table, the less likely. But what, really, would be the advantage of killing him?

When I drove out to the countryside the next day, in every bar I heard people crying out, "Rita did it, Rita did it." I was astonished. It was being alleged that Rita, Bob Marley's widow, had the most to gain from Peter's death. I have no idea whether it was true, but the entire island had a theory, and it sprang up instantly everywhere. What I do know is that Rita is now a billionaire living in Ghana. Marley, like Elvis Presley, is much more valuable dead than alive, in part because like Elvis no one else came along to overshadow him.

But I know nothing about this, nor would I ever expect inheritance to be a motive for murder or policemen to act as executioners. I only know what I saw that night. And I hear Bob Marley's song echoing in my brain: "How long shall they kill our prophets while we stand aside and look. They say it's just part of it, we've got to fulfill the book."

THE MAN WHO TOOK THE FALL

Somebody had to take the fall for the crime, so a minor figure associated with Peter was grabbed and charged. Dennis Lobban. He had just served a two-year cocaine sentence. He was short, slim, and had a very asymmetrical face, which did project some danger. He was said to have served the two-year sentence on behalf of Peter, who was guilty of the crime. It was also said that Peter had failed to look after the man's family while the man was in prison, a serious violation, and then failed to set him up upon his release — yet another violation. But none of this was true.

According to Peter's own people who inhabited a yard in East Kingston I visited, Peter never touched cocaine. The two years was the man's own crime. But Peter was a hard man. When the man emerged from prison he begged a money off Peter which Peter gave him, but when the man came back a second or third time Peter pointed to a vehicle on his compound and said, "You see that vehicle? If you want some money, go wash it for me." To which the man is said to have taken offense. But this alone was a trivial cause for such a crime, and he alone could not have gained entrance to Peter's home at night in Barbicon, since he was unwelcome and Peter did not tolerate fools gladly. This latter fact was well known; Chris Blackwell, the white producer of the Wailers, had always wanted to be liked by Peter, but Peter never liked him and always called him Chris Whiteworse. Not the sort of man to let Dennis Lobban into his home at night.

WHATEVER

The killings continue almost every day and many are heart-breaking. A tailor who has worked for thirty years in his shop in a humble district of Kingston at, I am sure, humble prices is shot dead one morning by two gunmen, for no

DENNIS LOBBAN. Is this the man that took down Peter Tosh? (File Photo.)

known reason. His twenty-eight-year-old son, just arrived, flings himself on his father and bawls out to him not to be dead. This was clearly not a father who had abandoned his son at birth like many others on the island. Or take a mere seventeen-year-old leaving home in search of a WIFI residence five doors down – murdered along with a twenty-one-year-old woman for completely unknown reasons. He looks like any old computer geek his age. His mother looks both frightened and in pain. Showing too much of her pain only makes her more vulnerable to the follow-up elimination.

How did this absurdity evolve, that an island famous for providing safe, sound tourist experiences for millions annually has become (outside these areas) such a dangerous place for its own people? As I mentioned elsewhere, the tropics themselves are conducive to murder, and the two political parties have adopted a ghetto mentality of organizing political districts into criminal ones enforced at gunpoint. But it's more than that. The ganja trade, initially conducted via numerous small planes landing on hastily-constructed runways, found it useful for both buyer and seller to trade guns for ganja – less cost to the buyer, more benefit to the ganja seller. And lately the U.S. has begun providing "monkey money" to the Jamaican Air Force in order to enable them to eradicate ganja by sighting crops from the air. Meanwhile the ganja-for-guns trade continues via Haiti, only now ships are likely to travel up large rivers such as the Black River, where transactions are completely out of view of the police.

So you might say that the high murder rate in Jamaica is just one more result of the very general and destructive U.S. policy of attacking other countries for its own drug problems. Mexico, Guatemala, Honduras and El Salvador all suffer grievously because the U.S. has a cocaine problem. Does this not violate the fundamental alleged logic of the U.S. economic system, namely that demand logically generates supply? So the problem with the U.S. attack on its neighbors is that it insists on punishing others for its own misbehavior – that is, supplying high quality versions of the very drugs the U.S. demands. If the U.S. has a drug problem it should attack the problem at its source, namely the user. Capitalism teaches that if you attack demand you have much stronger effects than if you attack supply.

But the whole hidden point of U.S. drug policy is to attack surrounding countries and enforce destructive policies on them. Coca leaves must be poisoned or scorched although the local people have a wealth of healthy interactions with this plant. Why? What is the economic return to the U.S. from Peru or Bolivia or all the other countries producing plants that are made illegal in the U.S. in spite of enormous appetite for them in the U.S.? That this produces violence is almost axiomatic. When activities with enormous economic effects are made illegal, all contracts within the industry, large and small, are ultimately settled at the level of a gun, since there are no courts. Police pressure in turn increases the level of violence as the police use the illegality to permit novel illegal violence of their own, generating its counter-response. A humble tailor falls dead in his shop, a teenager on the way to WIFI is killed before he can get on-line. These are the daily heart-rending examples of this insane toll.

CHAPTER 10

The Murder of James "Be-be" Bent

On February 18, 1988, I flew to Jamaica for a week of business connected with my scientific work on lizard malaria. I was primarily concerned to repair my research vehicle and to attend to some family business and, of course, enjoy myself along the way. February 19 was my birthday and the trip was planned as a surprise for friends and foes alike. Only my girlfriend in Kingston and two or three male friends there knew of my arrival. For the first time in my life no one in Southfield knew I was coming. The big surprise, however, was already unfolding for me in Southfield. Less than two days later, by early morning February 21, my closest male friend in Jamaica lay dead, his heart pierced by a knife thrust into the left side of his chest with such force as to break off its handle, leaving only the blade inside. James "Be-be" Bent was murdered before I got a chance to see him.

Be-be was a farmer and best known for running a ganja camp almost 24/7. That is, you could go to his home, an old-fashioned thatch-covered structure of stones and dried mud, and find him, usually with several others, consuming ganja or at least preparing it for consumption. If you wanted your own spliff it was available to you, but was more often consumed in a pipe shared by many. This was during the 1970s when Jamaica was under the Socialists, who had decriminalized ganja but forced on Jamaica an economic devastation so great as to invite treatment with the self-same herb. It was only years later that I considered that his running a ganja camp must inevitably have created some negative feelings in his neighbors because of the traffic it attracted.

In any case, for some reason I took to the man. He was very peaceful, warm and friendly, a loving spirit. He would talk to many people about their personal problems, especially the younger smokers. People he'd advised on a problem often described afterward a lightening of their burden as well as a lightening of the surroundings. But he also tolerated no slackness. He would not allow malefactors to smoke his pipe or join his camp. And he would directly challenge them, saying, "I don't want a tief or wrong-doer in my yard." He could partly get away with this style because he was very strong and skillful; people were not tempted to test themselves against him.

At first I was grateful to be in Southfield when he was killed, the better to grieve his loss with others. Far worse to learn of his death four thousand miles away in California, never to share the trauma directly nor to learn much about the actual circumstances of the death. But it was these actual details that soon came to trouble me and, in fact, set me off on a ten-day tear in which I ended up "investigating" the crime, sleeping two to four hours a night, smoking ganja continuously, and so polarizing the community that by the end of my stay some men were carrying guns against me, and I had to seek refuge in my lawyer's home. By then I had also had several physical fights, both in Southfield and elsewhere, including one in a Kingston night club that resulted in an icepick being shoved almost completely through my left hand.

Nor were the reverberations of Be-be's death limited to my stay in Jamaica. Within a month I was facing down twenty near-homicidal Germans in a bar in Seewiesen, Germany and, a week later, a German doctor bent on injecting a syringe full of tranquilizer into me as I was held by several orderlies in a Göttingen hospital. I declared that no "Nazi" doctor was going to inject anything in me, Germany still being an occupied country. Indeed, the amount he intended to inject would have put me in a coma for a week, if not a month. Soon I was speaking to a U.S. marine who wanted to know what the problem was. I explained the threat of over-medication, and I was soon set free, later to spend ten days in a mental hospital in Hamburg and still later ten days in one in Kingston. But all of that lay in the future.

"BE-BE IS DEAD!"

I arrived for my birthday visit in Jamaica on February 18, and was immediately swept up in the pleasure of reunions with people I hadn't seen in a while and who hadn't been anticipating my return. On the night of the 20th, I had a particularly enjoyable night and crawled into bed at about quarter of five. So I was surprised to hear my mother-in-law calling me awake shortly after seven. I knew that Miss Nini would never wake me at this hour for a trivial matter so I jumped right up. That was how I learned that Be-be was dead.

"How you mean?" I said. "How do you know he's dead?"

"The body went down to Black River a while ago and people are coming from the death yard now." As she spoke, she pointed to groups of people on the road drifting almost in a dreamlike fashion. Seeing them, I began to bawl out.

"Dead? Oh, my God. Who killed him?"

"Gladys."

Gladys was Be-be's girlfriend. They were not known to have the most harmonious relationship, but Be-be was so physically skilled he could easily have separated her from a machete without injury to either party. Indeed, he had often done this in the past. It seemed unlikely to me that Gladys could really have killed him.

I soon left for Be-be's yard and shall never forget my surprise upon arriving there to see not general sadness and funereal calm, as I expected, but an angry scene, a fracas of some sort, people shouting back and forth, even pushing, on two sides of an argument. What was unusual was the dimension of the contention: there were perhaps thirty or forty people involved, split into two warring camps. To me this resembled a dispute between two monkey troops or two matrilines within one large troop, and was undoubtedly organized along similar lines of kinship and affiliative relations. But why now, a mere three hours after Be-be had been murdered? And why here, within the yard of the dead man? I assumed that the fight had to be over the murder itself.

But it actually concerned goats. Gladys' ten-year-old son had appeared in Be-be's yard and started to lead off Gladys's three goats from Be-be's small

BE-BE'S GANJA CAMP. He is smoking, I am looking up. (Trivers File Photo.)

herd, intending to bring them back to his mother's yard. This seemed in it-self somewhat strange, making sure the killer's goats were separated from the victim's less than three hours after the murder. Stranger still was that when Be-be's son Junior intervened to prevent the removal of the goats, a youth named Donald had jumped in on the side of Gladys's son, laying hands on Junior and threatening him with a rock. Amazing. The father scarcely dead, his son already under homicidal attack, and the neighborhood split into two warring factions, apparently over goat distribution. This was starting to look less like an ordinary homicide and more like some kind of killing in a war between local sub-groups, or even the wiping out of a competing kin line, father and son alike. Better be careful, I said to myself, advice I did not take for a moment.

DONALD

In addition to the thirty or forty people in Be-be's yard, twenty or thirty people more stood massed together at the front of the house in Donald's mother's yard. As I strode into the yard and towards the group I raised both hands and said, "Peace, peace I come in peace; Miss Dee, can I come?" "Yes" from Miss Dee, Donald's mother. On the veranda of the house a youth of about seventeen was stretched out nonchalantly, maybe even insolently. As I approached, he bestirred himself and was identified to me as Donald. He was about five-foot-nine, muscular, apparently in good shape. "What business do you have attacking the son of a recently dead man?" I asked him.

Donald leapt down from the porch and told me to get out of the yard. I told Donald that this was not his yard but Miss Dee's, and as long as she gave me permission to remain, I would remain. I turned to her and asked if I had permission to remain and she said, "Yes." Donald now said that he lived here as well and ordered me out of the yard. I cannot remember the exact sequence of words that followed, but Donald and I were soon face-to-face, a few feet separating us, watched closely by all the people in the yard and at roadside. Again I asked him what business he had attacking the son of a recently dead man and, after a little back and forth, he said he had seen Gladys's son leading off her three goats when Junior grabbed hold of the boy and he, Donald, intervened to protect the ten-year-old at which point Junior grabbed a rock and Donald did likewise.

I then returned to Be-be's yard and questioned Junior. Junior said that Donald's account was almost, but not quite, accurate. He, Junior, had not touched Gladys's son but had laid his hands on the guide rope to prevent the goats from being removed. This had precipitated Donald's furious charge and Donald had laid hands on Junior. In response to Junior's defensive actions Donald had grabbed a rock, and Junior in turn grabbed one in self-defense.

My best friend had just been murdered and his son had been threatened with a rock to his head, and half the neighborhood seemed to support this. I could no longer do anything on behalf of Be-be but I certainly could on behalf of his son. It seemed there had to be some kind of communal hostility toward Be-be and his kin, and I intended to find out what it was.

THE DEATH YARD

The death yard itself had an unreality about it. Be-be's body had already been carted to Black River, and there was no mass of soaked or coagulated blood where his body had allegedly lain, nor anywhere else. Yet I had heard vivid descriptions of his blood bubbling up through his wound where his body was found. Someone had obviously cleaned up the death scene. Not only was the body quickly removed, as certainly made sense, but someone had gone to the trouble quickly of sweeping away evidence of where his blood had flowed freely.

I knew this phenomenon well now from my years in Jamaica. I had a good friend my age, Celestine, who ran a little grocery and bar. When I was on island we saw each other every week at her shop. Then one night she was murdered. She had been at her shop that night when the man arrived who rented her his jukebox. It was said that they'd had a sexual relationship. That night, he was there to collect his rent. Last anyone saw her alive, she was sitting sideways on his lap in his van in front of her shop. When he started to drive off with her still on his lap, she called out in a joking voice, "What are you going to do, a kill you a kill me?" Which is precisely what he did, striking her on the head repeatedly with a blackjack and then casting her dead body out of the moving van as if to make it look like an accident. Why he killed her remains unknown – lover's quarrel, quarrel over the jukebox rental, unchecked malice – the only thing that was widely known was that this was not the first murder he was associated with.

I had arrived at the scene of Celestine's death within ten minutes, but her dead body (as described by others) had already been removed and taken to the hospital. Shortly thereafter we discovered that the killer had smashed the vehicle in which the murder had taken place into a red road-bank, having cast Celestine's body out of the vehicle as if to make it look like an accident, and he was quickly surrounded by a crowd of people just a few dozen yards below the place where Celestine's body had been thrown. I was there and saw how members of the crowd, myself included, urged his death. He may only have survived because a relative of Celestine intervened to argue on his behalf, presumably in expectation of a later reward. The person who had grabbed up Celestine's body and rushed it towards the Black River Hospital was also aiding the killer.

MY ENCOUNTER WITH GLADYS BEFORE BE–BE'S MURDER

There is only one bar in Southfield. It's called Conny's and is where Little Man stabbed Jasper (see: Chapter 4). About twelve hours before Be-Be's murder, at around three p.m. on February 20, I ran into Gladys there. Normally if Gladys and I ran into each other at Conny's we would wind up against each other in mock sexuality; it was all harmless fun since, in fact, neither of us had any interest in the other and both of us were, in theory, friends of Be-be. But this time, for the fist time ever, Gladys held back when I approached her.

I noticed then that standing next to her on the other side was a tall, thin man. He was acting as if he had nothing to do with Gladys, and yet also paying close attention to our interaction. I continued to try to wind up against her in our usual vulgar style, and she continued to resist. So, testing the waters, I held out my arm toward the thin man, saying no one was coming between me and "my Gladys." No smiles, no pleasure from either party. Just two serious people who were clearly connected and obviously pretending not to be. Most curious.

Later, I was to learn that a skilled knife man had been brought from Kingston to kill Be-be, and that he was tall and thin. Was he the man next to Gladys at the bar and the reason she held back from our usual display? Who fe know, who fe seh? But I came to believe it, and, if I was right, it was one more piece of evidence that this was a carefully planned murder, financed by others, and not some kind of lover's quarrel gone horribly wrong.

GLADYS'S STORY

The following is the version of Be-be's death as Gladys wished it to be known. She and Be-be had had a dreadful fuss that evening, in which the house had been broken up, windows knocked out, and furniture turned over. Be-be had struck her with a rake and she had defended herself by thrusting a knife into his side with such force as to pierce his heart, leaving him dead on the spot. The police had asked her why she'd had to drive the knife in so hard that the handle broke off, and she had answered, "A flash, me did flash de knife, officer, and me nebber know how hard me did flash it."

The fatal wound had allegedly occurred not inside the house but on a small rise perhaps twenty yards from the house. She had then picked up his body in order to carry it out to the street, perhaps to get a passing car at four-thirty in the morning to carry her dying boyfriend to the Black River Hospital. The fact that the morgue for Black River is located on the grounds of the hospital made it convenient either way. She had dropped the body near an empty water tank and had gone searching for help. It was at that water tank that the body was found.

The man who found Be-be lying face down at exactly this spot, just off Be-Be's own property, turned Be-be over and one of Be-be's hands grabbed towards the wound. Be-Be said, "Unhhh!" and that was it, blood gurgling out of the side of his body and out of his mouth. His expression was the same as usual. No terror, no great pain, just the usual peaceful, calm expression with the pain of "unhh" added to it.

What was a bit at odds with Gladys's account of how Be-Be ended up bleeding to death near the empty water tank was that no one who saw her that morning remembered her as having any blood on her, much less being covered in it as one would expect after such a stabbing. Also, according to her story, she had made a remarkable series of quick trips once Be-Be had been stabbed, first to someone's house to get a vehicle to carry Be-be's corpse, then to another person's house to tell the news, and finally the most remarkable trip of all — she had walked a half a mile to search out a friend of hers and Be-Be's, apparently to tell him that Be-Be was dead.

Whenever I asked people, including her father, what Gladys's demeanor was like when she was taken away by the police, everyone said, "Just the same Gladys. Just the way she always acted." This was hardly consistent with her story of having just been involved in a violent struggle and putting a knife into Be-be with such force as to kill him with a single thrust. The notion that Be-be had used a rake against her was also hard to credit. He would strike neither child, woman, nor dog. In fact, he was widely considered overly passive and forgiving, perhaps as a result of too much THC coursing through his body. He'd once separated Gladys from her machete as she attacked, throwing each to opposite sides, without ever punishing her afterwards.

Finally, the direct evidence did not support the theory of a fight in the house. The glass from the broken house windows lay *inside* the house not outside the house, hence it could not have resulted from a fight *inside* the house bursting the glass outwards. It looked instead like a poorly executed attempt after the fact to create false evidence by beating in the windows from the outside.

"TONIGHT I AM GOING TO KILL BE-BE"

It is said in Jamaica that even the bushes have ears – even when you think nothing is around to hear you, someone may be listening. Since Jamaica is an island, it stands to reason that networks of sight and gossip are especially well developed.

I was to hear the most extraordinary piece of this strange story from my mother-in-law, someone not inclined to repeat random rumor. She told me that someone had been walking home about two-thirty or three on the morning of the murder and found Gladys crouching in the guinea grass on her haunches. When she called out and said, "Oy," the man called back and said, "Gladys, is that you?" She: "Yes." He: "What are you doing there?" She: "Is tonight I am going to kill Be-be."

Now, why would Gladys hide near where the murder was about to take place and call out to reveal her intention of killing Be-be? It suggests for one thing that the communal support shown toward her after the murder was not unexpected by her ahead of time. I suppose it's possible that murders are so extreme that they almost beg the murderer to share some of the pain. It's also possible that this story is false. But I do believe that Be-be's murder was premeditated and carefully orchestrated by Gladys.

HOW THE ACTUAL MURDER WENT DOWN

As near as we could tell, Be-be died in the following manner. His body had been found very near an empty water tank with no lip – that is, a large pit, which is easy to force someone into, and, once you do, you own him. As a result, people in Jamaica are often afraid to have a pit at their back. It cuts their mobility in half, if not more. Pits in the wild – often camouflaged – are used in the capture of large and dangerous mammals, rhinoceroses and elephants. As he turned the corner toward home Be-be was likely confronted by three men armed with machetes or knives. One of these was a skilled knife man. The three men would have forced him backward against the pit and killed him right in front of it.

Be-be was found with only one shoe. We soon found the other hidden in tall grass, hanging from a small piece of barbed wire on a fence about twenty feet from where the body was found. With his back to the pit, Be-be would have lashed out, and in the swirl of motion kicked his shoe some distance into the bushes. How else would it get there? According to Gladys she was carrying the dying man from his small house toward to road when, thirty feet into her walk, she dropped the body. It's hard to imagine anyone else hiding the shoe in such a strange place and fashion.

To those of us who mourned Be-be, the hidden hanging shoe was evidence of the final death struggle. A struggle that occurred right near the pit that he had to pass on his way home, and thirty feet from where Gladys had been seen squatting in the guinea grass awaiting his arrival. Whether she was there to call out and distract Be-be before his murder or was there merely to enjoy the spectacle we shall never know.

THE FATE OF GLADYS

There is a general rule in Jamaica that if you are quickly bailed after a major crime, you are going to go free. The case will be called up eight times over three years, thrown off for various reasons – documents or people not ready, previous trial too long – and finally, dismissed. But if they don't grant you bail – if they already love your company that much – you're going to spend some good quality time with them.

Gladys was bailed within one week by one of the biggest businessmen in town. There was long known to be bad blood between him and Be-be. Be-be used to preach against him in his ganja yard, and it was taken for granted that informers within the ganja camp brought back such preachments and condemnations to the big man. Gladys was never tried, nor was anyone else for the crime.

I saw Gladys about twenty years later, as we crossed paths on a backcountry lane. The two of us were alone, with no one else in sight. She was as ugly as ever, and as feisty too. I don't remember what I said to her, but I do know I cursed her roundly for her role in the murder of Be-be. She turned and yelled at me. Neither organism giving an inch on the matter. Just two animals on a trail snarling at each other over a long-distant event.

CHAPTER 11

Hanging with Huey

One of the few benefits of moving from Harvard to the University of California at Santa Cruz in 1978 was the chance to meet the legendary founder of the Black Panther Party Huey Newton. Indeed he was waved in front of me as a reason to come to Santa Cruz. He was a graduate student in "History of Social Consciousness" – roughly equivalent to Western Civilization – who had the wit to see that "social consciousness" started long before the Greeks and, in some form, by the time of the insects. He had gotten his undergraduate degree from Santa Cruz in 1974 and befriended Dr. Burney Le Boeuf, the celebrated student of elephant seals. Burney had been preaching the beauties of evolutionary biology – my own work in particular – to Huey, and so I had the good fortune of meeting him after he had already been well-primed.

I needed no priming. In the early '60s I had come to believe that African Americans should take a page out of Jewish history and murder those murderers of their own people who did not and could not receive justice in any other way. Just as the Jews had caught, tried, convicted, and executed Adolf Eichmann, I fantasized about a crack infiltration team doing the same in Mississippi to Byron de la Beckwith, who had murdered the courageous black NAACP leader Medgar Evers and then been duly acquitted by an all-male, all white jury in that state "drenched in racism." I had fantasies of doing so myself, but they were very short-lived ones – most likely I would not have reached the city limits before a cop pulled me over and said, "Let's see what this nice little white boy from Harvard has to say about the murder of dear old Byron."

So when I first read that so-called Black Panthers in Oakland were pa-trolling, and, if necessary, killing racist white police officers and appearing to get away with it I said, "Right on." And I say it to this day. Some deserve the death penalty, others multiple years in prison. I remain convinced that the Panthers were largely on the right side of justice.

THE TRICK OF THE PANTHERS

The Panthers began with patrolling the police. They would follow police at night or patrol until they came across police-citizen interactions. Huey might then emerge from a car with a law book in his hand and read out in a loud voice that, by law, "excessive" force cannot be used during an arrest. The police would invariably answer, "Our force isn't excessive." Huey would read them the legal evidence on that point. They would say, "Get the fuck out of here." He would answer that a citizen is allowed to remain within a reason-able distance of an arrest. They would say, "Your distance is unreasonable." He would flip to the relevant page and read the appellate ruling that declared a reasonable distance was ten yards or whatever, and it would go on like this.

Huey didn't invent patrolling police behavior. It was started by an L.A. organization called U.S. in 1965, but there was one critical difference in their approach: U.S. were unarmed. One night the LAPD beat all of them up, and that was the end of that. Huey was armed. He knew he had the right to be armed, and he knew he had the courage. So when he emerged from the car there was usually a gun beneath the law book so that, should the interaction turn hostile or threatening, he could be ready with a response. All this was legal back then, riding shotgun, in effect, on the police themselves.

During the war the Panthers waged between 1967 and 1973, roughly fif-teen officers died for every thirty-five Panthers. Not a bad kill-ratio when fighting the United States of America. I believe the Panthers had the largest single effect on integrating police forces in this country. The reasoning being: hey, if black people are firing at our officers, let's have some black officers firing back.

FIRST MEETING

Dr. William Moore called in the fall of 1978 to say that Huey, who was then in prison, charged with beating up a tailor in his home for calling him "boy," wanted to take a reading course from me. I said that was fine but I wanted a paragraph from Mr. Newton on what he wanted to read. Before he could reply he was released from lock-up and traveled to Santa Cruz to meet me. We met at Dr. LeBoeuf's home. Huey was accompanied by Dr. Moore, his aide-de-camp Mark Alexander, and his bodyguard Larry Henson. When he told me that he had spent three years in solitary confinement, I asked him if he'd ever feared or endured a mental breakdown in all that solitude. He described a night when his whole psyche seemed to fragment and tear apart and he had to struggle to hold himself together and fight the fragmentation. This he acted out, with strong arm muscles acting to compress some exploding object. So we formed a strong psychological bond on the spot. I had suffered the fragmentation and collapse, he had fought it off, and he was open about it.

By the way, if you had a feeling for "vibes" (as Californians called it) you could feel Huey shivering as he sat talking. This was a result, I believe, of his having just come out of two months of the male-male hell that is prison.

We decided to do a reading course on deceit and self-deception, a subject I was eager to develop and on which Huey turned out to be a master. He was a master at propagating deception, at seeing through deception in others, and at beating your self-deception out of you. He fell down, as do we all, when it came to his own self-deception.

A DAY WITH HUEY

Shortly after that first meeting at Dr. LeBouf's house, I was invited to Huey's home for our first class together. This is hardly how it would have gone with any other student. But this wasn't any other student, so I drove to Oakland and spent seven hours in his home as his guest, the intensity of the situation leavened by the presence of his beautiful wife Gwen.

Huey Newton was certainly one of the five or six brightest human beings

I have ever met. Each of those five or six has had a different sort of intelligence, and Huey's forte was aggressive logic. While you had to lean over to hear what Bill Hamilton was saying, sometimes you would be blasted against the back wall by what Huey was saying. And he moved his logical sentences as if they were chess pieces meant to trap you and render you impotent. "Oh, so if that is the case, then this must be true." If you moved away from where he was pushing you, he would say, "Well, if *that* is true, then surely so-and so must be true." So he was maneuvering you via logic into an indefensible position. The argument often had a double-or-nothing quality about it where, in effect, he was doubling the stakes for each logical alternative, giving you the unpleasant sensation that you were losing more heavily as the argument wore on, making more and more costly mistakes.

The shortest form of this argument could be called the "Huey two-step," as in the following. Huey was angry at me one day for allowing myself to be described in a popular scientific magazine article as knowledgeable about both cocaine and marijuana prices on the streets of Montego Bay. It was a mistake to mix the two, was Huey's contention; one was enough. And since I was already widely associated with marijuana, which in turn had numerous redeeming qualities, Huey felt I should not be publicly associated with cocaine. Of course he was right. So I came up with some feeble argument about how if it was useful to others to know this fact (though I had no reason to suspect it would be) then the cost of self-revelation to me didn't matter. Almost like Jesus volunteering to be tortured on the cross. To which he replied, "In that case, why don't you lecture naked?" Newton two-step. Argument over.

Speaking of cocaine, I was naïve enough that, during that first independent study session at his house, I never noticed the white powder around his nostrils, nor how often he left the room and returned. I was only told later that he stayed up the whole night before our visit, snorting cocaine throughout, as his wife begged him to get some rest and not destroy another important meeting. Cocaine was Huey's drug and his downfall, but in this case I think it only buzzed him enough to overwhelm me – indeed, I had to take my customary nap before heading back down the road. He made me take the nap in his own bed while all was silent throughout the house. That was Huey Newton: if you were his guest in his home, you came first. That was the warmth of the man. As for cocaine, at that time in Oakland it was known as "the dancing lady" and you were warned, "Mind that she dances off with you some night."

After that trip, my wife and I had them down to Santa Cruz and shortly after he arrived, having already mastered the basics of evolutionary logic, he took me aside and said, "There is only one thing we might disagree on – do you believe in free will?" I answered that I didn't know what people actually meant when they used the term but that I believed organisms had the ability to look back on their actions and decide whether they wanted to repeat them. He embraced me. We apparently disagreed on nothing.

MY FIRST NIGHT OUT WITH HUEY

The next time I saw Huey we met for a men's night out – me, Huey, and two of his top guards, Larry and George, set out to hit a few clubs in West Oakland. We ended up at a very pleasant club, filled with people of both sexes, and we had plenty of laughs and fun interactions with the larger crew, but, as would happen so often, we stayed too long. The club thinned down to us at a table and three drinkers at the bar. Huey called for a final drink. It was 1:50 a.m.

The waitress came back to say that it was too near closing time (2:00 a.m.) and she couldn't serve him a drink. He told her to tell the bartender that he wanted a drink. She returned to say that the bartender couldn't do what he'd asked, since it was closing time. Larry and George got up and stood by the front door and the door to the men's room, each unbuttoning his jacket. Huey now walked up to the bar and said, "If you don't serve me I'll knock this place over." Wow, I thought, this is getting exciting. I'm about to be the getaway driver on an armed robbery! I later learned that knocking the place over meant robbery of the entire club, including all its patrons. There was a deep silence. Then a tall, thin, gray-haired, light skinned, African-American man of perhaps seventy spoke up: "Well serve the man a drink!" Brilliant stroke. Problem solved, bartender busy at work, Huey back in his chair.

The drink arrived. Huey had a five-dollar bill to cover the two dollar cost.

No, it was on the house, said the waitress. No I insist, said Huey. No, no, no, no — no charge for your drink. Huey insisted, the five dollars went on her tray, he drank the drink and we rolled on out.

I felt great. Huey explained the details of what we'd just been through to me as we roared off laughing. Fast departure because you never know when reinforcements will arrive. Absolute necessity of paying for the drink because in the eyes of the law if you accept a free drink under threat of armed robbery, you have committed armed robbery.

Huey incidentally was an expert in the law, especially misdemeanor law. His familiarity with the field began with his father, who taught him that the police use misdemeanors to catch you in your felonies, so you had to pay close attention to misdemeanor law. His father also taught him that you can take a killing but you can't take a beating and warned him to avoid, "Liars, thieves and gamblers."

The importance of attention to misdemeanor law was brought home to me very forcefully late one night when we were driving around in West Oakland, me at the wheel. Huey told me to turn around, so I made a U-turn. Immediately, he began to berate me: "It's illegal to make a U-turn within the city limits." "But it's three in the morning." "The law applies 24/7." "But there's nobody around to see us." "You don't know that. You only know you can't see anyone." He proceeded to instruct me on the proper move, which was to turn left into someone's driveway and back out facing in the opposite direction.

So misdemeanors were off the table. And if he was committing a felony, he always warned you. Sometimes he would get in my car and say, "I'm dirty." This meant either that he was carrying a gun or a quarter pound of cocaine. He carried each on a couple of occasions with me. In one case we were on our way to see some ex-Party members who were now into cocaine full-time in West Oakland and lived in the Acorn apartment complex. In the Acorn complex, you were in danger of being robbed on the way in and robbed on the way out. Either way, this put both of us in jeopardy. But I had chosen to become a Panther as a mere foot soldier; Huey was dominant and so I rolled with Huey. We were not robbed and no police officer ever stopped us. One of Huey's legs was a bit shorter than the other and Huey could exaggerate the resulting limp so people would see quickly it was Huey Newton arriving with security in the form of me.

AN ARMED ROBBERY LEADS TO PROTECTING
CHILDREN ON THEIR WAY HOME
FROM SCHOOL

According to Huey, the Black Panther Party started as a simple, old-fashioned robbery, which he was planning with a number of confederates. Problem was he was reading Franz Fanon and becoming politically conscious. So he decided to use the robbery to start a new political party, as radical as its start-up funds. The hard part was selling it to his fellow robbers. They didn't like the idea. "They almost killed me," Huey told me, but finally he got them to sign off on it, and some of them even became Party members later.

Huey liked to tell me that there was nothing quite like the thrill of a bank robbery. He would act it out, coming around the corner with his gun drawn and pointed unerringly at his intended target, all while announcing the robbery in a calm, authoritative voice. When he was planning a bank robbery on behalf of the Party, a federal agent apparently overheard him telling his men, "Don't worry about messing up, because if you do I'm going to kill you."

Once, when he and I were driving through West Oakland, near Berkeley, Huey pointed out the site of the Party's first political act. There was a street corner at which local African-American children were run over nearly every year while attempting to cross one particularly dangerous street near their school. Numerous requests had been submitted for a stop sign and a proper street crossing to protect the children. Nothing had been done.

One day the Panthers appeared at the street crossing at the appropriate time, dressed in their leather jackets and berets and each carrying a rifle or shotgun. They proceeded to direct traffic, standing in the highway to permit safe passage for the children. Six weeks later the city put up not a stop sign but a stoplight at that very corner. Nothing like armed black men to stir civic activity. At least in Oakland. In the Louisiana of their birth they would have been assaulted, arrested, and a few killed in the bargain.

GUNS AND BLACK PEOPLE

Huey was a master of visual imagery in its many forms. "Wanted: Dead of Alive" posters featuring a policeman, named and pictured: "Must be presumed to be armed and dangerous at all times." A poster of himself, seated on an old colonial wicker chair, an African spear in one hand, an American rifle in the other, Panther beret on his head, and a serious, straight look on his face. As if the Party were a new colonial power come out of Africa, one that was using what had helped so many others colonize the world – guns. When the Oakland police shot up the poster in the window of Party headquarters, Huey simply made another poster out of that image; it showed so clearly what the police would like to do to him were they not constrained by his Party, his fame, his financial backing, much of it from Hollywood, and the legal power that it bought. All you need to produce is "reasonable doubt" and a little planning can go a long way.

When the California legislature was meeting to decide whether to pass the "Huey Newton law," as it was popularly called, which stated that you could no longer "ride shotgun" but instead had to keep your loaded gun in your locked trunk, Huey and thirty five other Panthers showed up in Sacramento on the day of the vote, most of them carrying rifles. They tried to enter the legislature with their guns, which was allowed by law at the time. Police stopped them from entering, ordered them out of the building, and shortly thereafter arrested them.

Huey told me that many black people argued against the public display: "Now they're sure to pass the bill, why don't you ease up the pressure?" Huey's response was simple: they were going to pass the bill anyway, and he wanted to show black people that they had the right to show up in front of the legislature with guns and confront a mass of armed police. That was one of the main points of the Party – to encourage African Americans to use their right to bear arms in self-defense. It was in response to a lynching that

HUEY IN A WICKER CHAIR. (*opposite*) Posing both as a colonial and an armed revolutionary. (File Photo.)

President Harry Truman made the first and key decision in favor of equal gun rights for the black man in the U.S. when in 1948 he integrated the armed services. Before then Black soldiers sliced the carrots and did the dishes.

Many African Americans of more recent times have a strong ambivalence or hostility toward Huey and the Panthers because they believe he helped spawn the culture of black gun violence among the urban young. There is probably some truth to the charge, but I think harsh drug penalties take a larger part of the blame. With the stakes so high for being caught selling illicit drugs, the chances of internecine war and murder inevitably rise as well.

To those who make this charge against Huey, I would also ask what alternative they'd propose to black gun ownership. I suppose you could have armed whites all around disarmed black cities, therefore suffering no internal gun strife, but we have in fact gone through that period. Remember when a howling mob of armed whites burned the thriving black business community of Tulsa, Oklahoma to the ground in the 1920s, killing scores of black people in the process? To be the only unarmed people in a country built on armed violence is not a good position.

Another point I'd make to Huey's detractors is to remind them that the Panthers helped usher in the wholesale integration of police forces throughout the country, and certainly in Oakland where the Party started. And while it is certainly true, as Huey pointed out, that painting a cop black does not in itself make the cop any better, still, in principle, the black cop is likelier to know how to judge whom from whom and is less likely to have racist attitudes toward his own kind.

A final point on Huey's legacy: though people tend to assume that Huey was anti-police in principle, in fact he saw obvious value to community surveillance and organized protection. That's why he regarded himself and Party members as on a par with the official police. He used to joke, "I've got nothing against the police as long as we are firing in the same direction." When he met Palestinian leader Yasser Arafat, Huey asked him why he had to use random acts of terror against Israelis. Arafat replied that it was because he had no other weapon. Huey said, "Well in that case, ok." But Huey himself never believed in random acts of violence. His violence – whether for good or evil – was always highly directed and specific.

ANIMAL IMAGERY

Huey had an extraordinary, intuitive understanding of animals and animal imagery. Although he was not the inventor of the following usages, he seized upon them and popularized them: "Black panther" for black revolutionary and "pig" for a police officer.

Nothing as black at night or as terrifying as a panther. And pigs have a long, distinguished history of being unclean because of a parasite found in their meat. Personally, though, I've always had a fondness for pigs. They're very bright. Few things are cuter than a family of bush pigs running across the high grass of the African veldt, father or mother in front and rear, everyone with their tails raised high, presumably the easier to follow. To see them tied to stakes and forced to root and live in a small space for their entire life is painful to me, though not nearly as painful as the grotesque way in which our "food industry" has produced conditions of mass torture unheard of even in our prisons – chickens, cows, and pigs unable to turn around for their entire life.

Huey once mimicked a moose giving its territorial defense call when challenged – a deep rising moaning sound. He said that he had brought out the moose call in me when, during an argument over splitting royalties evenly, he had suggested that instead of one-third to him and two-thirds to me, as we had originally agreed, it should be two- thirds to him and one-third to me. And I do, indeed, remember the feeling of territorial invasion that seized me, as if suddenly being attacked on two sides simultaneously. And there was a "moose" quality to my voice, as I said, "Wait one minute there, Huey!"

When his wife caught him returning from a three-day bender and was blistering him, he would imitate to me his response in front of her, head down, his paws raised to his chest and hanging limply while he said to her, "It's the dawg in me, honey; it's the dawg."

The following is not quite animal imagery though it is close. Huey routinely used to refer to "your black ass" in a conversation – this without regard to your ethnicity or color. Once he caught a look in my eye because he leaned forward and said, "Bob, *all* asses are black if you look closely enough."

I soon adopted the style as my own, which led to a fun minute one evening

HUEY WITH NATASHA. His wife Gwen is behind them. (Photo courtesy Jay Frieheim.)

HUEY AND ME, SAME DAY. In the afternoon party at my home. (Trivers File Photo.)

with a young African American graduate student at Santa Cruz with whom I was arguing. I made reference to my own black ass, at which point he stepped forward and said "*Whose* black ass?" I stepped forward and said, "*My* black ass." He stepped back and said, "Your black ass?" I stepped back. "My black ass." Problem solved; once we knew whose black ass was in play, tension abated quickly.

Huey was beyond racism, certainly way beyond my own. There were Asian and white Panthers from the beginning; I was only a late example. I naively assumed he would show a bias toward the darker side. Not so. Huey was the Godfather of my slightly darker-skinned twin daughter Natasha, and he once took me aside and said, "Don't let your racism against white people cause you to discriminate against your lighter skinned twin, Natalia." Guilty on both accounts. He himself was a quarter Jewish through admixture from the rape of his then sixteen-year-old grandmother by the son of the man employing her mother, and he always respected that side of himself, despite its ugly origin. He would sometimes remind me that he was a quarter Jewish, knowing full well that I was almost half – as if to say, and if you want to compete with me in this area, go right ahead.

DUMMYING UP

We normally think of deception where self-image is concerned as involving *inflation* of self: you are bigger, better, or better looking than you really are. But there is a second kind of deception – deceiving down – in which the organism is selected to make itself appear less large, less threatening, and perhaps less attractive, thereby gaining an advantage. Being less threatening to an individual may permit you to approach more closely. The most memorable instance of deceiving down that I learned about was when Huey Newton taught me the Black-American term "dummying up." This refers to a tendency to represent yourself as being less intelligent and less conscious than you actually are, usually the better to minimize the work you have to do. So an employee may dummy up in order to avoid being required to do more difficult things. In Panama, I routinely saw many instances in which the

Spanish-speaking people would misrepresent themselves as understanding less English than they did or as being considerably less intelligent than they actually were, all in order to gain benefits from the benighted *gringos* who all too easily believed the dummying up.

One day I asked Huey how he dealt with dummying up by others. As head of a large organization he must have repeatedly faced this problem among his underlings. It took him a while to catch on to what I was asking him, but when he did his whole face lit up and he became animated and said, "Oh, you want to know how I handle *that?*" He then launched into a brilliant verbal attack on an imagined example of dummying up. I only wish that one of Richard Nixon's aides had been on hand to silently activate a tape recorder so that none of this was lost to posterity. Unfortunately, I can only give a rough sketch of Huey's answer.

If I remember correctly, he imagined a situation in which a waiter is always managing to position himself so as to avoid seeing his boss calling him and to otherwise appear to be working while not actually doing any work. His own monologue in response to this ran roughly as follows: "Oh, so you're so dumb that you happen to be looking the other way whenever I'm trying to get your attention. And you're so dumb that when you know I *am* watching you, you decide to polish silverware that needs no polishing. And you're so dumb that you are always walking toward the pantry without ever reaching it. Well, you're not *that* damn dumb!" – followed perhaps by slapping the organism to the ground, verbally or otherwise. In short, Huey revealed to the actor the hidden logic of his actions, and the final ironic punch line was that, "You're not that damned dumb" since you've managed to arrange all this dumb-acting behavior in such a coherent pattern, designed to deceive your employer.

HUEY'S DARK SIDE

Huey had a dark side that he did his best to hide from me. He was largely successful in doing so. I never really saw his dark side in action. I heard a few mild stories from him, but it was only from others that I learned of the dreadful deeds done within the Party for infractions of the rules. Huey was the Minister of Defense, which also turned out to be the Supreme Court. All death penalties had to be approved by him, which was the same thing as saying that only he had the power of the death penalty.

Did he kill Kathleen Smith a, seventeen-year-old prostitute working at San Pablo and Twenty-Eighth Street early one morning in 1974, after she called out, "No little punk is going to tell me how to run my street corner"? It was widely believed in the community that he had. Her alleged words could not have been better fashioned to bring about her end; punk was a prison term and Huey had spent more than three years in prison for apparently killing a racist white police officer, so "little punk" would not strike him as an appropriate greeting at four in the morning. At that time he was trying to organize the usual criminal enterprises – prostitutes, drugs and protection – to serve Party ends. Also he was a dead-eye shot according to everyone in a position to know – he drew, he aimed, you dropped. I've always chalked this up to purity of intention. If I throw a stone at a dog, I often unconsciously fear retribution and so at the last minute pull the shot off center. Not Huey. If he wished you dead, you were dead.

Another gruesome incident I came to hear about involved a woman, a Party member, who developed an attraction for, and began a sexual relationship with, a woman already involved in a sexual relationship with Huey (who was himself married). The new woman had not asked Huey's permission for the affair, which he would almost certainly have granted – then he would have asked to join in. But did the penalty for starting a lesbian relationship on the sly have to be being beaten nearly to death, with permanent damage to her backbone? Surely not, but this is precisely what happened. The job was assigned to a physically imposing party member, something of a legend himself, who later pled guilty to manslaughter. Incidentally, when that man emerged from thirteen years in prison, he devoted his life to helping the poor, the downtrodden, and other ex-prisoners re-integrate into normal life.

I don't know how to reconcile the warm, brilliant man I knew with these brutal acts, except to say that perhaps having the gall to attack and kill white police officers in Oakland and to threaten to do so throughout the country requires a certain character consistent with cruelty. Certainly he had both the gall and the cruelty. He planned and carried off the execution of particular

officers. He brutally beat and sometimes murdered people of various ethnic-
ities, and often for no crime at all. I will say I did not detect much sadism in
him, which is more than can be said for one of his top guards whom Huey
himself warned me to be careful around because he enjoyed causing pain.

Recently we have had an extraordinary spate of police killings of African-
Americans youths under the flimsiest of pretexts: a child waving a toy gun
in a store or in a park – boom, dead on the spot. Yes, indeed, where are the
Panthers when we need them most? Huey did not believe in punishing the
whole community, as in burning down South Central Los Angeles because
three racist cops had been exonerated for beating up dear old Rodney King.
He believed in justice, not in two innocent cops executed sitting in their
squad car in Brooklyn as happened the other day in New York City, just because other cops had seen fit to execute citizens in broad daylight via choke
holds or straight shootings.

Huey believed not in killing police at random but in assassinating officers
worthy of the sentence. He would not have advocated killing the officers
who beat up Rodney King, since Rodney survived, making his beating less
than a capital crime. He would have felt differently, though, about the execution of a twelve-year-old child playing with a plastic pistol in a Cleveland
Park two seconds after a police officer arrival – that was a capital crime.

I was a Panther myself for three years before Huey "ex-communicated"
me one memorable night and told me to stay out of his "territory" by which
he meant Oakland. It was for my own good he assured me, and I believed
him and still do. I was going through a manic phase that was upsetting fellow
Party members who would have gladly gotten rid of me if I weren't known
to be very close to Huey. But this, in turn, put an extra burden on him. So
it had to stop. One joke back then was that you never stopped being a Black
Panther. It was like the Mafia – you could only exit by death.

THE KILLING OF HUEY P. NEWTON

On August 22, 1989 Huey Newton was shot to death in Oakland, California
at 5:50 in the morning outside a crack den. The shooting was done by one

Tyrone Robinson. They were said to have spoken briefly. Then Tyrone turned to leave, but he only took two steps back before he pumped three bullets into Huey's head. Huey may have been harassing him for a hit but Tyrone, recently released from prison, was a member of the Black Guerilla Family, a prison gang long at odds with the Panthers. Tyrone may have thought he would rise a notch in the organization by killing Huey, and he may have been right. But his own relatives turned him in, and he was back in prison within a day.

I was in Jamaica and learned of Huey's death the next day. It was six in the morning and I was in Black River catching female and juvenile common lizards while they were still sleeping – it being very hard to get them when they're wide awake and active later in the day. When we arrived at Black River, I bought a newspaper, flipped to page three and saw a picture of my friend. Oh my God, I thought at once, a dead him dead. No other reason for his picture that I could imagine.

Later that day, a telegram from my wife arrived: "Huey shot dead." I went back to my property and carved his initials and date of death into a slow-growing, long-enduring cactus tree. Not much more to do. I had neither the resources nor the interest to fly to his burial, nor anyone in Jamaica with whom to share my grief. Huey was gone.

The last time I saw Huey was on the twelfth floor of the criminal justice building in Oakland, two months before he was released and four months before he was killed. We were separated by glass and talked over phones as we faced each other. He had served two and a half years in prison and was about to be released, at last paying his "debt to society." We had been chatting for a while when he asked, "When was the last time you hit the pipe?" I assured him it had been several years. Then I said, "I guess you're going to be free for about twelve minutes before you hit the pipe. "No," he said, his head snapping hard to the right and back again. There was a pause and then a smile. "Too fast, eh?" he asked. In our work on deceit and self-deception we had noted that lies could either come more slowly than the truth – as the brain took time to invent the falsehood – or too quickly. When they came too quickly it was because of denial, a wish to sweep the truth off the table with a single word: "No!" He was indicting himself. And, sure enough, three months later he was shot dead outside a crack den.

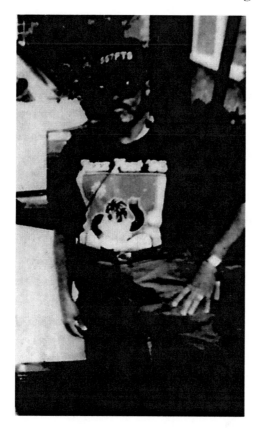

MELVIN NEWTON IN JAMAICA. In 1996 when he changed my inscription of Huey in my cactus tree. (Photo courtesy Robert Trivers.)

I think he knew it was going to end like this. His great autobiography was titled "Revolutionary Suicide." He'd chosen the phrase, he told me, because it captured what he'd always believed would happen to him. He was sure he would be shot to death in the course of the armed struggle to discipline the racist, white police. It would be suicide, in a sense, but with revolutionary implications. He called the other kind of suicide "reactionary suicide."

He often told me he was surprised that he hadn't died in the Panthers' war against police in the late '60s or early '70s. Some Eastern religious figure had once warned him that after all he'd done and been through, a full two-year meditation program was mandated, but this was something he was not about to subject himself to. So ironically he committed reactionary suicide at the end. Not directly, but by pursuing a lifestyle destined to lead there. The dancing lady had indeed danced off with him. What pain he bore from all the hurt he'd inflicted, from all the denial he'd endured, I cannot imagine.

Eight years after he died, his brother Melvin visited me on Jamaica and saw the cactus memorial I had made. He told me that I had done it wrong. I should have carved in his birth date as well as his death date. I did so, and we were treated at once to an extraordinary sight. First the arrival of the Doctor Bird – the male scissor-tailed hummingbird – flitting about, and then, and almost immediately, there appeared a God Bird, female of the species and very rarely sighted. It was almost as if Huey were alive, only in some other dimension.

CHAPTER 12

Under Arrest

Being under arrest is never pretty. Each arrest has its unique qualities, but what they all have in common is an abrupt reversal in fortune, complete loss of freedom, often in novel and unpleasant surroundings. Your survival itself may be at stake. Other arrestees are apt to be on the aggressive and unhappy side, just as you are, and all-male confinement does not tend to induce pacifism, nor warm communal love.

I have spent over a year of my life in lock-up due to being bi-polar. Often when I'm brought in by the police during a manic episode, it's obvious that I need to be incarcerated in a hospital, and the transfer promptly takes place. Getting out once you're in requires some negotiation, as well as evidence that your manic phase is sufficiently under control. After the episode is indeed under control, you suffer a depression of a half to a full year, after which you are back to functioning as you were before. This subject would almost require a whole book in itself, but here I am skipping it entirely and focusing only on my criminal arrests.

For this account, I have simply gone through my arrests in the order in which they occurred. Most are trivial, over in less than a day but some are more serious. The worst were the ten days I spent in lock-up at Half Way Tree in Kingston, Jamaica.

ARREST IN NEW MEXICO FOR MULTIPLE DRIVING OFFENSES

My friends and I were driving from Albuquerque, New Mexico, to El Paso,

Texas, summer of 1962, in order to cross over into Juarez, Mexico, for a night of fun. It was Friday and we had all come off construction work building the University of New Mexico's football stadium.

It was a four-hour drive. After a couple of hours, impatient with the current pace, I asked to take over the wheel so that, "An Easterner can show you Western boys how to make good time on a highway." We were soon hurtling down the road, a good twenty miles over the speed limit, crossing the double "no cross" lines in the middle of the road in order to overtake other cars (this maneuver being made safer by the high over-all speed) and in general going all out for El Paso and Juarez.

Everything was going well until I happened to glance in the rearview mirror. "Jesus Christ, look at that fool!" – half a car-length behind us at eighty miles an hour! Then I noticed that a light was flashing on top of the vehicle: a police officer who had, as he soon informed me, been following at that distance for six full miles. So I was the fool. Had I not noticed him, he wanted to know. No, I was too busy driving. He grunted. Of course given the way I was driving it was unsafe to take one's eye off the road to check the rearview mirror. But, alas, breaking multiple laws while driving made checking the rearview mirror all the more advisable.

"HAVE THESE BOYS BEEN DRINKING?"

Soon enough the officer noticed that we had been drinking. There were six cans of beer unopened and six opened and sucked dry. Who of us had bought the beer? The man stepped forward. Was he twenty-one years of age? Yes, he was. None of the rest of us were, and we were not allowed to drink. "Have these boys been drinking," the officer asked?

"No, they haven't."

"I'm going to ask you one more time – have these boys been drinking?"

"Yes, they have."

Fastest conversion to truth I have ever witnessed in my life – and a very wise one at that.

"I'm glad you said that, because if there is anything I hate it's a liar, and if you had lied to me one more time, I would have hung you from the highest pole in New Mexico." The officer then took me in his own car, up front, to the local courthouse. I was under arrest but none of this unpleasantness of handcuffs. My friends followed behind in their pick-up. The case took no time. The Mexican-American judge sized me up and fined me thirty-five dollars. I had thirty-seven dollars on me, so she was compassionate. She left me two dollars for Juarez. We ended up sleeping in a park in El Paso from four a.m. to daylight.

On the way home (with someone else driving) the back wheel came off and actually passed us, picking up speed without the burden of our vehicle on top of it. While we, of course, shuddered toward the shoulder.

RIDING ON SUSIE'S HOOD

My next arrest occurred not more than thirty yards from my apartment, during a party I was throwing in Cambridge, Mass. What happened was this. My ex-girlfriend Susie was presuming to leave my party about two a.m. Having just laid on my back and chug-a-lugged Jim Beam bourbon in front of everyone, I was reluctant to see her leave so soon. I followed her downstairs in all good spirits, but placed myself in front of her Porsche, as if preventing her from moving. She took me up on my challenge, and I soon found myself on the hood of her car, looking for safe purchase. This was provided by her dual side rear-view mirrors, a novelty at the time, each of which I grabbed.

Susie continued the joke by driving around the block. Apparently someone seeing what appeared to be an assault underway, bravely thwarted by a woman driving a Porsche, called the police. After slowly rounding the final corner to home, a police car screeched around the corner after us, its sirens screaming. Susie pulled to a halt, I jumped off and was made to spread-eagle while I assuring them, "I am unarmed, officers."

They were not inclined toward pleasantries. No amount of begging, pointing out that Susie and I were old friends, my apartment now only thirty yards away, and I was sure to stay inside if they only permitted me to, had any effect. I was arrested and my girlfriend was given a ticket that read, "Driving with an obstructed view of the roadway, man on hood" – or, as my friends later put it, "Hood on hood." A police van was called and I was duly transported to the city jail.

I do remember being given my one phone call. I called back to my friends at the party, who thought I had run off with Susie. I remember speaking very reasonably – "The officers feel it would be better if I spent the night here," and so on. I was locked away in a cell by myself for the night and the morning's catch revealed three others, two winos and an eighteen-year-old who had been found driving a car he had no papers for.

The officers treated everyone well except me. The winos were given some wine from their stash confiscated the night before. They gave nothing to the car thief but treated him civilly. To me, they were openly hostile. Why, I wondered to the young man? "You don't remember what you were yelling when they brought you in here last night?" I did not. "You were cursing them left and right, calling them mother-fuckers for holding you for the night."

I still have no memory of this, but I can only imagine that I really had expected that a little old-fashioned charm and respect would get the officers to permit a friend to pick me up so I could spend the night back at my home – and my party. And that when that failed, the real me – fully drunk – came to the fore. I'm surprised they didn't beat me!

UNDER ARREST BY THE GUARDIA NACIONAL IN PANAMA CITY

In 1980 I had a prestigious fellowship from the Smithsonian and space provided to do a year of tropical research in Panama, living in Gamboa in the middle of the old Canal Zone, which was at the time in the process of being returned to Panama. I did do some tropical research on ants and moths, which was what I was ostensibly there to do, but not much. I had a full parental burden – four children under six years of age – which I promptly augmented with a night life in Panama City.

One night my nephew and I were caught up in a "drug sweep" on Avenida Central in Panama City. This was when the Policia National would grab six or seven on the street, sometimes at random but more often targeted, as this almost surely was against me. They then search you for drugs, looking especially for small packets of cocaine. When they opened your wallet they appeared to take sadistic pleasure in jabbing into each corner while watching you for any sign of fear. None from me, brother. We had, in fact, been trying to score some earlier but fortunately we'd failed. No marijuana on us either. So they released my nephew, but escorted me to their new headquarters where they held me as I watched them process new prisoners. I was not under arrest so much as "detained."

After I had spent a while sitting and watching bookings, some officers appeared with a giant set of Klieg lights, arranged in rows, with which to examine my car. Those that stayed behind watched me for signs of nervousness while I prayed the entire time to be calm and serene. The chance that they would find even a seed was negligible since my nephew had given the car a good Jamaican cleanup before we set out. Jamaica was a country in which any evidence of marijuana could earn you eighteen months at hard labor, so clean was clean.

But they returned with a bizarre exhibit. They had my ashtray, within which was what looked like the end of a marijuana joint, except that it was not burned at either end. I reached for it. They drew back. Then I heard something most remarkable: "This time, no problem. Next time, no problem. Third time, problem." They seemed to be giving me a free sin since I had passed what was essentially a set-up.

A U.S. African-American prison guard later gave me the insider view. The sudden drug test in downtown Panama was a set-up originating from a conflict I had had with the old U.S. Canal Zone police over overtly racist behavior that my bi-racial family was experiencing in Gamboa, a "white" town in the old racially segregated Canal Zone. A police officer had told my wife, when I was out of town, "The best thing for Dr. Trivers would be to take the first flight out of Panama," a threatening remark if I'd ever heard one. So I'd met with him and his commander under the instruction of the Smithsonian, to make clear to the man the implications of his statements. Of course he denied making the statements in the first place.

Since these police could no longer act directly against me, they got their brand new Panamanian officer friends to help out (this was during the three year transition into-full Panamanian sovereignty), hence my detainment in Panama City. If this theory was correct, it may have explained the unusual free offer from the Panamanian police – you have done nothing against *our* laws; if you were singled out unfairly by the gringos we give you one free pass in our system.

DUI IN CALIFORNIA

I was arrested for Driving while Under the Influence in California, and they were dead right. I was drunk and they had every right to arrest me in the name of public safety, my own included. I was tooling down 101 from Oakland to Santa Cruz at about three in the morning, having had a full evening of attempted psychosexual interaction. It was late at night and time to go home. I was so drunk I kept hitting the bumps installed between lanes. By the third such bump a police car signaled its interest in me. Since I couldn't even find my license and registration in my over-stuffed glove compartment I was arrested on the spot.

I had three choices. I could give them a breathalyzer, urine sample, or blood sample. Although breathalyzer was the least intrusive, it seemed a bad idea at the time. I was drunk and an instantaneous test would quickly reveal this. Blood was out of the question; far too much personal information stored in that medium. That left urine, so I signed up for a urine test.

I spent the next forty minutes in the back of a police cruiser, hands cuffed behind my back, while they filled out all the necessary paperwork, which turned out to be considerable. Then they drove an hour to the Alameda County Jail and processed me for another twenty minutes. This long delay turned out to be very advantageous.

On check-in, they found a little bindle on me in which small amounts of cocaine, a gram or two, are often stored. What was I doing with this, they wanted to know. In fact, I had brought it with me from Santa Cruz to store exactly what they suspected, but I had failed (fortunately) to make a buy. But this was not my pre-arranged story. I was an entomologist, I told them, and occasionally encountered important insects while on the road. These bindles, I had found, were uniquely useful for storing specimens, keeping them quiet and undamaged. Not a single officer believed me, but the lie allowed me to look them in the eye and give a narrative. Meanwhile, one cop could not control himself and licked the inside of the bindle, undoubtedly hoping for a hit. This bioassay did confirm absence of cocaine while obliterating any evidence that might have existed.

I was now taken for the urinalysis. I was told first to empty my bladder fully. I couldn't believe my ears. If Jesus had appeared and sanctified me I could not have felt more blessed. I was about to let out two gallons of sixty percent alcohol, leaving something much milder for the after-urine test, which they duly bagged and preserved for later testing. The long first piss also gave me the opportunity to flush a quarter ounce bag of marijuana from my jacket that I *had* managed to buy.

Unfortunately, I wasted all that luck by then doing something stupid. I was made to sit in a chair while an officer facing diagonally away across the room filled out more paperwork. I felt around in my pockets and uncovered about four roaches, the final partly-burned pathetic dead-ends of joints, kept by poor people such as myself when that is all they have. This itself would lead to a marijuana charge so I searched myself carefully, while unbeknownst to me the officer watched my every move out of the corner of his eye. Suddenly I tossed all four dry joints in my mouth and started to grind away. He immediately leapt up and seized me by my throat, preventing me from swallowing about half of the macerated roaches.

"What did you throw in your mouth?" he asked. "Something I want to swallow," I answered. He ended up carrying away a tiny chewed up ball, so that later when the urine evidence came in that I was only 0.08% alcohol, the legal limit, they could jack the charge up to driving under the influence of "alcohol and drugs," which would have subjected me to the same consequences as a drunk-driving conviction. Later they claimed to have lost the material for THC testing and I was let off with a $400 fine for "dangerous, dry" driving, which means driving poorly but not due to drunkenness or under the influence of drugs. Exactly opposite of the truth, of course.

In any case, that night I was put in a cell with several other men and, periodically, the guards opened the door to allow in two more prisoners at a time. These new men were invariably bare-chested and dropped every two minutes to the floor to do twenty push-ups before continuing to prowl around the cell. The officers were giving the rest of us a glimpse of what awaited us if we elected to spend more time in their company.

I rested the night on one side with one eye open. In the morning I was let out, and they pointed me toward a bus stop a half-mile away, at which I might find transportation to bring me to where my car had been towed. I later made the return trip safely with much less alcohol in my blood than on the start of the trip.

TEN DAYS LOCKED UP AT HALF WAY TREE, KINGSTON

The longest I have been locked up in a jail was ten days in Kingston, Jamaica. It's one thing to be locked up in your own country. There you know the rules, you have ready access to help, and you know how to contact lawyers and their value. But being incarcerated in a foreign country is another matter entirely. One day you're staying at the mighty Pegasus hotel, backed up by your debit card, the next day you're locked up at Halfway Tree Station nearby, charged with "credit card fraud." You have no idea what your "rights" are in this country, especially in this situation. You do not have the phone number of a single of the three "big men" in Southfield who might be inclined to pay your bill and free you. You don't know a single available lawyer or even how much good a lawyer might do you. What you soon learn, though, is that the felony of credit card fraud carries the potential penalty of a nine-month sentence in a Jamaican prison.

Here's how it happened. In the spring of 1996 I was staying at the Pegasus for two days. The Pegasus is a large, posh hotel in the heart of New Kingston that is sixty percent government-owned. At that time there were two rates for the same room – the foreigner rate of $300/night, or the local of $100/night. Since I had married a Jamaican woman in 1975, I had the right to the local rate. I also had a Jamaican driver's license which itself required that I have a tax identification number for Jamaican tax purposes and so on. Open and shut case. I had only ever paid the local rate on this island, most recently two months earlier at the Pegasus itself.

This time was to be different. Having been at the hotel two days, I returned to my room to find I was locked out. My key no longer worked. Certain that this was a minor error I went to the lobby, only to discover that I was locked out of my own room for failure to pay the room bill. It had now ballooned to $1000 for two days and my debit card, now accessed by them for the first time, showed no such value. At no point in the discussion would they allow me to broach the discrepancy between the $100 per night I owed and the $300 per night they'd charged. Nor would they allow me access to my own room, which happened to show that three months earlier I had paid the Jamaican rate at the very same hotel. After some delay I was duly arrested, accused of the felony of credit card fraud (though how this could be carried off using a *debit* card was beyond me) and jailed at the local facility on Maxfield Avenue at Half Way Tree.

Ten days I was to spend in lock-up over the relatively trivial matter of which rate should be applied to my hotel room bill. Had I been in a better state of mind, I would surely have gone the high class route of saying, sure, we have a difference of opinion about the rate, but hold on to this debit card, and my passport as well, and on such-and-such a date my monthly salary will hit the account, at which point you can draw out your money and I can pick up my card and my passport, while referring the whole matter to my attorney. But I went the low class route: No, you are locking me out of my room with the evidence that disproves your position, fuck you. Nothing makes a madman madder than a living contradiction.

I was given my one phone call, but knowing no lawyers in Jamaica, nor friends' numbers at that hour, I called an attorney in the U.S. who failed to heed my pleas that he find me a Kingston lawyer next morning, guarantee payment, and get me out of jail while we adjudicated the matter. The next morning I had not a penny on me, no phone numbers, none of my family or friends in the U.S. knowing I was locked up. Only a recent friend from Cornwall Mountain in Westmoreland to wonder what kind of situation she had blundered into when what was supposed to be a pleasant stay at a Kingston hotel had turned into her friend's incarceration.

When I was taken into lock-up, they skipped the first floor and took me up to the relatively luxurious suites on the second deck. They stopped in front of a cage of young men, perhaps eight or nine cramped into a small space, seething with energy and aggression. Fortunately my warders moved me one cell to the right and I joined five older men in a cell built for four. Two of them were in their forties so immediately it was a more hospitable setting. There was only one young man among them, well-muscled and pacing.

There were two sets of bunk beds made out of steel – that is, flat slats on which you could rest, the floor being much colder. Since there were five or six men in our cell, some of us had to sleep more than one to a "bed." When it came to you to share one of these beds, as it did to me, you slept with legs scrunched up to avoid touching your partner, who slept similarly scrunched up.

Later in my stay, I came to realize that I was really in the prison equivalent of business class. If you continued to the right down my cellblock, cells went from reasonably bad to surprisingly pleasant. That was first class. At the very far end was a cell with a couch and a soft chair, where a single occupant could often be seen reading, sometimes attended to by the guards. The advantage, presumably, of money and social status.

I only found out how bad the downstairs cells were when they led a group of us through there one morning when we were on our way to appear before the judge. Here there were cells on both sides of a main corridor, most of them covered by burlap bags and occupied by many more than our own cells – twelve or fifteen to a cell, mostly youths in their teens or early twenties, cramped into the same small space. They acted like monkeys when they saw us, shuffling together in our shackles: jumping up and down, calling out, insulting, beseeching. On each side of the cells were culverts that ran down the middle and were supposed to carry waste matter downstream; we had separate bath-stalls that we needed permission to visit. So this was a real piece of hell – stinking rank, over-populated and over-caged, all male, all the way. Knowing from some experience that in this situation no response at all was the best strategy (in the language of evolutionary theory, no response was an ESS – an evolutionarily stable strategy) we hunched forward, said nothing, and slowly made our way out and on to court.

The food was even worse than the sleeping arrangements. If it had meat in it, the meat was spoiled, rendering the entire stew inedible. One morning they announced callaloo and I thought this boded well. Callaloo is a Jamaican specialty, a cross between collard greens and spinach. It's full of vitamins. I didn't expect thyme or other spices, but I could not see how they could mess it up, so I went down and got myself a big slop of it. But it was way too salty and they gave us no water to wash it down. They were clearly acting spitefully, deliberately wasting resources so as to inflict pain. Salt costs money, after all. Along with the callaloo came some white puffy rolls but my fellow inmates warned me that this was where the staff hid the sedatives, so if you wanted a nearly comatose prison experience, polish off nuffa rolls. I don't know if this was true, but I'd had enough sedatives forced on me in my lifetime, and I didn't eat them.

It was with bitter irony that later, free of captivity and living in the outside world, I read an outraged article in the island's one major newspaper, *The Gleaner,* decrying the fact that, according to the published budget of the prison section of the government, each prisoner was being fed better than the entire lower quarter of the island. This is in a countryside where a few yams and mangos may easily see one through rough times. We were, of course, being fed far below this minimum. But since the entire Jamaican budget was known to be a fiction, as money was drained off from project after project, did anybody really expect the government to protect monies meant to care for prisoners?

JUDGE MCINTOSH

I was later to learn that my judge, Judge McIntosh, had a well-deserved reputation as one of the cruelest judges on the island. I was certainly astonished by his perverse cruelty. I remember one occasion when he appeared to offer leniency at first, immediate release to a West African youth for overstaying his visa by some seven months, a trivial offense, only to turn around a few days later and sentence the same youth to two years in prison. It hurt us all. We went from congratulating him – you soon reach Ghana! – to saying nothing at all (him soon reach hell).

Of course, I was due a little respect as a white man and an American citizen. When I said I had no attorney and had been given no chance to call someone to help, the Judge pointed to a rather attractive dark female police sergeant and I said, "Whaaa....!" which brought down the house, but that is all it did. The woman never contacted any of the people back in Southfield whose names and phone numbers I gave her and who could easily have bailed me out.

Here was my daily routine while in that Kingston jail. I was taken out of the cell block around seven a.m., manacled to other prisoners due in court that day, and marched to holding cells near the court, where our handcuffs were removed and where we were soon enough joined by various prisoners from police stations throughout Kingston, Three-mile, Six-mile, Greenwich Town, Rollington Town, and so on. These were usually younger men, full of energy if not aggression. This was not a trivial trip in their lifetime. We were about to appear in court in our own cases. We all preferred a slightly raised ledge against one wall, the better to see out of the single slit window.

Throughout the morning we were taken out of the cells and into the courthouse in small groups, and held in a holding area adjacent to the courtroom. I was always last or second to last in line, so sometimes it was after one p.m. that I entered the court from the holding area to face the judge, having eaten not a thing for over twenty hours and barely able to stand upright. As my fellow prisoners mimicked it, this was how our daily interaction went:

McIntosh: "Do you have zee money?"

Me: "Den how me fe have de money, sah, den nuh me a prisoner sah?"

McIntosh: "Hold him until tomorrow's Court."

THE POCKET BIBLE

If one of us had not had the pocket Bible – four Gospels, Psalms, Proverbs, and Ecclesiastes – I do not know what we would have done. At least once a day if not more you would beg it from its owner, study a psalm of a prayer or whatever, and return it to him. We even had Sunday services. One person read from the Bible, another gave a prayer, and a third gave a thought for the day. Only thing we lacked was a Choir, and we sure would have liked that. I sometimes carry the pocket Bible on me, and if people ask, I say I am only being prepared for possible confinement. My favorite is Ecclesiastes, almost every line fitting some aspect of my life, though few as closely as 12:12: "Of making many books there is no end and much study is a weariness of the flesh."

When then-Governor George Bush mocked a born-again Christian in prison as merely a "jail-house conversion" I saw red. This is a popular lie in some circles, that prisoners find Jesus in prison in order to influence the parole board or, in this case, the Governor himself. Slim chance. Bush had never served a single day in jail, in spite of traffic and cocaine offenses, always protected by his family name. He was said himself to be a born-again Christian, but he had not yet learned mercy. The woman whose religion he mocked had not directly harmed a soul. She was a member of a group of about ten people, two of whom were responsible for killing two people during a robbery. On the theory of joint responsibility, she was convicted of felony murder and sentenced to die, while the two killers received life without parole.

Bush had no intention of commuting her sentence to life without parole. From that time on I felt he deserved to die, and in 2000 I knew a deeply dangerous organism had been elected to lead the "free world". And when the U.S. invaded Iraq in 2003, and Bush had to sign off on airstrikes in and around Baghdad likely to have significant civilian damage, he signed off on every one. So there you have it: the pseudo-Christian incapable of showing compassion for a woman with minimal criminal responsibility decides to punish the wrong country in the wrong way in the wrong region for the wrong crime.

Trust me, if you cannot find Jesus, Mohammed, or Moses in prison, you can't find them anywhere. One reason you will find God Almighty in prison is because you need God – there sure as hell is nobody else looking after your interests. And you need something positive to focus your mind on while in confinement, someone who is inside the cell with you but outside as well.

Other than religion, the second most useful thing to have in jail was money. As long as it wasn't jacked off you by a fellow prisoner, you could use it to buy phone calls, food, and cigarettes. Every evening several inmates were allowed outside their cells while the rest of us were locked in, and they would come running by calling, "Two with a box for forty!" (Two in a cigarette box.) Or, "Two alone twenty," "Two in a wrap thirty" – the prices would often decline as the evening progressed, so that you could get a full box with two for only twenty dollars. The extra prices for the boxes and the wrap showed the poverty of prison – you had no place to put your property, so a cigarette box was an item of value.

Having no money, I lived off the kindness of the older men, all of whom were there on minor cocaine charges, and each of whom had a wife or girlfriend bringing in food as well as cigarettes. These men were my salvation. Each shared a bit of his dinner with me as well as his cigarettes, and there is nothing like captivity to increase one's desire for a cigarette. Much more so than weed or stronger drugs, nicotine is a direct survival-under-pressure chemical. They also advised me to remain in our cell during the daytime, instead of joining those roaming about. Better to stay in one's own cell, meditate, read the pocket Bible, and avoid interacting with a set of younger men.

THE DAY OF MY RELEASE

The day I was released was the day my nephew showed up with the $1,000 to pay for the hotel bill. The judge accepted the money and promptly found me guilty of "credit card fraud." Jamaica is perhaps the only country in which using your debit card permits you to be convicted of "credit card" fraud. The fine of $100 was promptly paid and I was released, with cellmates in many cells that I'd not interacted with reaching through the bars to touch me and wish me safe journey until I was out the door.

When I emerged after ten days of lock-up, I had lost twelve pounds. I looked like what Jamaicans call "crawny dog" – that is a scrawny dog, all ribs showing. I also emerged a nervous wreck, unable to dial seven digits on a phone in front of me; someone else had to do it for me. This was not because I was molested in prison or threatened in any way. An occasional shoulder into shoulder or verbal threat, but nothing serious.

The older prisoners had advised me well to avoid the false illusion of greater freedom in the larger cage that was open to us every morning. Although larger in space, it had relatively more caged men, younger and more aggressive. That was an invitation to conflict and cost – and for what? Was there anything of value out there except an increase in bodily motion in space, something you could easily achieve in your own cell? Perhaps one of the reasons push-ups are so popular in jail. Nor was my confinement solitary. Each cell was designed to be smaller than the number of its inhabitants and most of us had no visitors at all and so we came to depend upon each other for company.

No, what had so degraded my mental and emotional state was ten days of lack of food, lack of motion, lack of freedom – with the overhauling threat of incarceration in prison in an all-male world. I did not go into lock-up in the best of conditions. I came out far worse.

I like to believe I had compassion for prisoners before this ordeal, but I know I have strong compassion for them now; some deserve to be in there, and many do not, but for all of them it is a rough life. I often feel that way about animals in captivity, too. Not just chimpanzees, but pigs and chickens and God knows who all. Being tied up or hemmed in, not permitted even to turn around in your whole life, that's not what natural selection has been favoring these millions of years.

But selection has also not favored complete deprivation of all human contact – nor all contact with nature. The U.S. Constitution bans "cruel and unusual punishment," yet fails to see how unusual it is to scientifically construct an environment entirely devoid of much of the sensory stimulation humans evolved to require. That this is also extremely cruel is obvious upon inspection.

CHAPTER 13

Vignettes of Famous Evolutionary Biologists, Large and Small

Some of the following people are well worth remembering for their great achievements and the way they did them; others are not. But all were well known in their time and today, and some exercised undue influence. I have already described the parallel cases of Ernst Mayr and Bill Drury. Bill was the most important influence in my life but, unlike Ernst, barely known to the outside world. Each of the following are people who influenced me in some way at some point in my life to a greater or lesser degree and for better or worse.

RICHARD DAWKINS

I first came to know Richard in the following manner. I was in Jamaica on sabbatical in 1975 when I received a letter from one Richard Dawkins enclosing a paper written by himself and Tamsin Carlisle pointing out that I had committed the Concorde Fallacy in my paper on Parental Investment and Sexual Selection – as indeed I had. The Concorde Fallacy is the notion that because you have wasted ten billion dollars on a bad idea – the Concorde – you owe it to the ten to throw in another four in hopes of making it work.

In poker, the rule is, "Don't throw good money after bad." Good money is money you still have, bad money is already in the pot; it is no longer yours. Just because you have $300 in a large poker pot (money gone) does not mean that you owe it to that money to lose another $200, with odds stacked against you. Every decision should be rationally calibrated to future pay-offs only, not past sunk costs.

I had argued in my paper that since females almost always begin with greater investment in offspring than do males, this committed them to further investment – they would be less likely to desert their offspring. Simple Concorde Fallacy; only future pay-off is relevant. I consoled myself with the thought that there probably was a sex bias similar to the one I'd proposed, but only because past investment had constrained future opportunities. In any case, I wrote back that I agreed with them right down the line.

I soon received a second letter from Richard, saying that his actual purpose in writing me was, in part, to find out if I might be willing to write the foreword for a new book he had written called "The Selfish Gene." This was especially appropriate, he told me, because my work, more than anyone else's, was featured in his book. What the hell, I thought, and he sent the manuscript along. There were indeed chapters based on individual papers of mine – "Battle of the Generations" (parent-offspring conflict), "Battle of the Sexes" (parental investment and sexual selection), "You Scratch My Back, I'll Ride On Yours" (reciprocal altruism). I never deluded myself that my work was more fundamental than Bill Hamilton's, nor did Richard, but we both knew that if you wanted to get some of the fun details filled in on a variety of subjects – not ants, fig wasps, or life under bark, but social topics relevant to ourselves – my work was a better bet than Bill's.

In addition, Richard had a most pleasing combination of absolute mastery of the material with a wonderful way of expressing it – funny, precise, vivid. Let me give one example. He presented Bill Hamilton's idea that a gene – or a tightly linked cluster of genes – could evolve if it could spot itself in another individual and then transfer a benefit based on the phenotypic similarity. But Richard added a vivid image, calling this "the green beard effect." The name soon caught on in the scientific literature, so that everyone today (even when talking about bacteria) will refer to "green beard" genes. The phenotypic trait is obvious: you have a green beard. And the genetic bias is obvious: you favor green-bearded individuals. Genes spread apace. Except what about a mutant that leaves your green beard intact but takes away your bias toward green-bearded individuals? Not at all obvious, yet Richard's vivid way of writing facilitated thinking through the complexities.

So I said to myself, yes I will write you your foreword, though I don't know you from Adam. I wrote a good five paragraph foreword but it consumed about a month of my life, partly because I actually like to think before I write, which does slow down writing – but so do massive doses of THC. In any case, once I was finished, I looked at the essay with dismay. I had managed to chastise our pseudo-Marxist friends, by saying they were "counter-revolutionaries" while we were the true revolutionaries, at least where underdogs were concerned – children, women, and the lower half of the social order. Still, how could I have wasted so much time over such a trivial task for so little effect? Could I not squeeze any self-benefit out of this endeavor?

Why not slip in the concept of self-deception, I thought, whose function by that time I had linked to deceiving others? This I regarded as the solution to a major puzzle that had bedeviled human minds for millennia. And Dawkins, bless his soul, could hardly have set me up more nicely by emphasizing deception in his book: "…if (as Dawkins argues) deceit is fundamental to animal communication, then there must be strong selection to spot deception and this ought, in turn, to select for a degree of self-deception, rendering some facts and motives unconscious so as not to betray – by the subtle signs of self-knowledge – the deception being practiced. Thus, the conventional view that natural selection favors nervous systems which produce ever more accurate images of the world must be a very naïve view of mental evolution."

Perfect and not even in a paper of my own but in someone else's book and an incredible bestseller at that. And sure enough, in 1979 Richard Alexander produced a version of my argument so Dawkins gave me priority for an idea I regarded as a fundamental insight into mental evolution, unappreciated until that moment. I've always felt grateful to him for this. Indeed at the time he was kind enough to congratulate me for adding a fresh idea to his book. It was only in 1985 that I laid out the argument in more detail. But I did it in a thirty-five-page chapter in a textbook on social evolution, and almost no one reads textbooks for new ideas so it remained dormant for another twenty-five years.

I did downgrade two of his ideas that I later came to value. Memes are non-genetic elements that spread because they are imitated. I wanted the genes more in control. A gene that propagates a meme immediately propagates it to those without the gene so meme/gene interactions are expected to be complex at the outset.

But recently I have come to like the concept. We have at least good quantitative data on memes replacing each other without any obvious genetic bias. "Sex" has been replaced by "gender," first in the humanities and the social sciences and now in biology itself (David Haig) as the term we use to refer to the sex of an organism, where sex refers to whether the organism produces eggs or sperm/pollen. "Gender," by contrast, has for centuries referred to the sex of words rather than organisms: amigo, amiga are different genders of the same word. Indeed, there are languages in which genders of words have nothing to do with sex – kidneys are masculine, lungs are neuter, the liver is feminine, and so on. I believe what lies behind this change is a desire to minimize the biology, as opposed to the sociology, of sex differences. If the words we use for sex differences refer only to the words we use for words, then cultural and environmental factors loom larger. But there is an irony here since we are now witnessing a time of multiple genders, not sexes, and "trans-gendered" individuals. I have softened somewhat my opposition to this verbal trend.

Another nice example of Richard's memes in action is provided by the so-called euphemism treadmill proposed by Steve Pinker. You begin with a euphemism – say, "toilet," itself originally meaning "towel" as in make-up and primping. But then it's so associated with its new meaning that it comes to imply what you wish to hide, so you need a new euphemism. "Toilet" becomes "bathroom," so you are bathing in there, but that is a bit personal, so it becomes a restroom, and you are taking a nap in there. Memes are changing in an orderly fashion. This is going on all around us. Janitors become Custodians. Operators become Information Assistants. God knows how bad it gets in the middle and upper reaches of bureaucracies. More recently I have seen that memes are usually more powerful the more unconscious they are. Even the euphemism treadmill is partly unconscious, but it is the memes of race, religion, class, and nationality that are the more potent ones. Here are likely to reside deeply biased (semi- or completely) unconscious memes with strong individual and group effect.

Richard also went on to emphasize the "extended phenotype," an idea I also downgraded at first. The concept is obvious. Most birds build nests, and if you come within a foot of me and have a sense of smell you will know I have an extended phenotype too. His book on the topic was an excellent review of the subject. Very few people know that parasites have evolved to manipulate our behavior to their benefit. Parasites whose next stage is a fish-eating bird have evolved to cause the fish they are in to swim near the surface, sideways, which increases the chance the fish will be eaten by the parasite's very own next stage host. And for all you know, when you are just coming down with the flu – no real symptoms but highly contagious – you naturally stand two inches closer to people at a cocktail party than you otherwise would. But what did the term "extended phenotype" add to the discussion?

Recent work on the evolutionary theory of cancer (Paul Ewald) suggests that the concept of extended phenotype has quantitative and conceptual utility that I hadn't seen. Consider a tumor. It evolves in a micro-environment that consists of the larger organism. In this environment it evolves new tricks to manipulate the larger host to its own reproductive advantage. Tumor cells need nutrients and blood flow as much as do other cells – in fact, the more malignant they are, the more they need. The tumor does not evolve these structures itself of course – it is a one-generation wonder – so it expropriates those produced in its microenvironment by the larger organism. In the language of Dawkins, it extends its phenotype so as to include a series of blood vessels to support it. The tumor also benefits from extending its phenotype through several different kinds of tissues, including cellular barriers partly evolved against it to end up in a cellular matrix within which the cancer can evolve to have positive effects on its own propagation by manipulating some of the many chemicals in the matrix.

When I learned that Dawkins had taken on religion in the name of science and atheism, I felt he had finally found his true intellectual niche. No way could they keep up with Richard. I was starting to give the Tinbergen lecture at Oxford on June 13, 2011, when as usual I misplaced something on the lectern and muttered "Jesus Christ," which the microphone amplified to the four hundred people in attendance. I then looked up and said, "I hope Richard Dawkins is not here." Richard raises his hand. So I congratulate him for putting up free-thinker signs on the London bus system, something I did admire, and they were so mild, things like "There is probably no god. Now stop worrying and enjoy your life." Or later, from a child's perspective, "Please don't label me. Let me grow up and choose for myself." So for the audience I added, "I regard Richard Dawkins as a minor prophet sent from God to torture the credulous and the weak-minded – for which he has a unique talent," as indeed he does. One nice concept in his book on atheism is that since most people dismiss all religions except one – why not go the final step?

W.D. HAMILTON

I thought of Bill as perhaps the greatest evolutionary theorist since Darwin. Certainly, where social theory based on natural selection is concerned, he was our deepest and most original thinker. His first work, in 1964, which outlined his theory of inclusive fitness, was also his most important. It is the only true advance since Darwin in our understanding of natural selection, and an inevitable extension of Darwinian logic. The idea goes like this: because parents are genetically related to their offspring, increases in reproductive success are reflected by increases in some gene frequencies in nature. But we are related to our full siblings as much as to our children, so if a gene were to appear that caused us to increase the number of our siblings at a cost of the loss of almost as many children, that gene would spread. A noteworthy implication of Hamilton's work is that in almost all species, an individual is no longer expected to have a unitary self-interest, because genetic elements are inherited according to different rules, with a man's Y chromosome going only to sons while the X goes only to his daughters along with mtDNA.

The idea that genetic relatedness going sideways, e.g. between siblings or cousins, might have profound implications had been briefly advanced by R. A. Fisher and J. B. S. Haldane, but neither took it seriously and neither provided any kind of mathematical foundation. That foundation was not as

ME AND WD. Bill Hamilton and I are teaching a course together at Harvard in spring of 1978. (Photo courtesy Sarah Hrdy.)

obvious as it sounds. For a rare altruistic gene, it is clear that $rB > C$ will give positive selection, where B is the benefit conferred, C the cost suffered and r the chance that a second copy of the altruistic gene is located in the recipient by direct descent from a common ancestor. But the matter is not so obvious at intermediate gene frequencies. As the altruistic gene spreads, should not the criterion for positive selection be relaxed? Hamilton showed that the answer is "no," and that his simple rule worked for all gene frequencies.

He once told the story of sitting down as a doctoral student to write to Haldane with some questions, but to formulate each question more precisely he had to do additional work, and after a couple of years he never sent the letter because by then he'd worked out all the answers himself.

He followed his first work with major advances in understanding how selection acts on sex ratio, senescence, the aggregation and dispersal of organisms, and even reciprocal altruism. Bill then devoted himself to the theory that parasites play a key role in generating sexual reproduction in their hosts, with recombination being a defense against very rapidly and antagonistically co-evolving parasites. In his memorable phrase, sexual species are, "guilds of genotypes committed to free, fair exchange of biochemical technology for parasite exclusion," as augmented by mate choice, especially for parasite-resistant genes.

All great minds have their unique style and Bill Hamilton was no different. While Huey Newton would blast you against the far wall with the force of his argument, you had to lean in to hear what Bill was saying, so soft-spoken was he. It was almost as if he clutched his thoughts close to the chest. But the effort on your part was well worth it. His every thought on every topic rewarded close attention.

In 1969, Bill came to Harvard to lecture. He was coming from a "Man and Beast" symposium at the Smithsonian in Washington, where he had presented some of his latest thinking on spiteful behavior in an evolutionary context. This was the same talk he'd be giving us. There were perhaps eighty or ninety people in attendance, almost filling the lecture hall, and most of us were there with eager anticipation. Hamilton got up and gave one of the worst lectures I had ever heard in my life.

For one thing, he lectured for a full fifty-five minutes without getting to the point. The material was abstruse and technical; he often had his back to us while he was writing things on the board; you had difficulty hearing his voice; you did not get an overview of where he was going or why he was going there. When he realized that he was five minutes over time and still hadn't gotten to the point – or indeed very near it – he looked down at Ed Wilson, his host, and asked if he could have some more time, perhaps an extra fifteen minutes. Of course Professor Wilson granted more time, but he also made a rolling "let's-try-to-speed-this-up" motion with his arms. Hamilton then called for slides. The room went dark, and there was a rumble and a roaring sound as about 90% of the audience took the opportunity to escape. I remember walking home with Ernst Mayr, both of us shaking our heads. It was obvious that the man was brilliant, a deep thinker, but whoa, was he bad at public speaking.

Hamilton was not unaware of this problem. He once told a class we taught together at Harvard that after hearing him lecture many students would doubt that he understood even his own ideas. He did improve considerably in subsequent years, but he still showed the touch of a true master. Once, as a guest of the Institute for the Study of Law and Behavioral Sciences, lecturing to a group of law professors, he introduced a trick that I had never seen before. He showed a number of interesting but complex slides on parasite-host interactions. He had a hand-held microphone but no pointer, so he used the microphone as the pointer. Often all you would hear him say was, "Here, as you can see..." and then the microphone would point to various parts of the slide while his mouth continued to move. Then you might hear, "And then in the next slide..." and once again you would not hear anything about the slide, though you could see Dr. Hamilton pointing animatedly to various places in it with his microphone while moving his lips.

My first impression of Bill was that he was physically strong. I remember thinking that if the argument ever turned physical, the contest I would least like to be engaged in against him was a shoving contest. He once returned to Oxford from Brazil with cuts and bruises sustained when a man tried to steal his wallet while brandishing a knife, and Bill chose to fight him off. I felt that he would dig in his heels, you would be unable to move him, and he would lean forward and shove you slowly and stubbornly to wherever he wished to get you. Intellectually I imagine the interaction may have gone along similar lines.

It is hard to capture on paper the beauty of the man and the reason that so many evolutionists felt such a deep personal connection to him. He had the most subtle, multi-layered mind I have ever encountered. What he said often had double and even triple meanings so that, while the rest of us speak and think in single notes, he thought in chords. He was modest in style, with a warm sense of humor. He once sent me a news item on a father to son testicle transplant with the comment, "New vistas for parent-offspring conflict?" The last time I saw Bill, at Oxford in December 1998, he pointed with pride to the two, possibly three, species of moss growing on his Volvo – indeed on its front windows – and told me that this was a clear advantage of Oxford over Cambridge, the latter being too dry.

I was in the UK to give the "Darwin Lecture" at LSE in 1998, apparently the last ever. Bill introduced me and in the course of his introduction said that until recently he did not think self-deception was biologically possible. I thought to myself, "Were you raised in a closet? How can you reach your age and not notice self-deception or give it some emphasis?" But now I think that this is part of a larger rule that applies to me too: those very strongly devoted to the truth are especially vulnerable to a certain level of untruth.

He certainly had one of the most creative minds I have ever met in biology. I still remember the day a graduate student came running down the hall saying, "Have you heard Hamilton thinks that bacteria use clouds for dispersal?" As quick as you can say "Bill Hamilton," I asked, "Has he shown how the bacteria get the rain to fall where they want?" And indeed it was so. His idea humbled me because ever since I had been going to Jamaica, I'd heard rural people say, "Trees draw rain" – as in, don't cut them down. And I had thought to myself, "You poor benighted souls, you have the correlation right but causality wrong – naturally, where it rains more, trees are more apt to grow." Now Bill was suggesting that Jamaicans may well have been right all along – lower temperatures over wooded areas could itself be a useful signal to rain.

Bill Hamilton was a naturalist of legendary knowledge, especially of insects, but he was also an acute observer of human behavior, right down to the minutiae of your own actions in his presence. Had I noticed, he once asked, that lopsided facial expressions in humans are usually male? No, I hadn't, but I have seen it a hundred times since then. Bill died at the age of sixty-three on March 7, 2000, from complications after contracting malaria during fieldwork in the Congo in January, work which was designed to locate more exactly the chimpanzee populations that donated HIV-1 to humans as well as the mode of transmission. This was in service of a theory that HIV-1 spread into East African children via polio vaccination. I regarded this theory as doubtful from the outset, and now it's been firmly disproved. So, in one tragic sense, he died in the service of trying to prove a falsehood. But he was strong in mind, body, and spirit, with many new projects and thoughts under way. He has been sorely missed ever since.

STEPHEN JAY GOULD

I first met S. J. Gould when he was a freshly minted Assistant Professor in Invertebrate Paleontology at Harvard and I a graduate student in Evolutionary Biology. Invertebrate Paleontology was well known then as a backwater in Evolutionary Biology, eighty percent devoted to the study of fossil foraminifera whose utility was that they predicted the presence of oil. In this environment, it was obvious that Gould would go far. New York City Jewish bright, verbiage pouring from his mouth at the slightest provocation, he surely would make a mark here.

This was not why I was visiting him. I had heard he was an expert in 'allometry' – indeed had done his PhD thesis on the subject. Back then I wanted to know everything in biology, so I sought him out. Allometry refers to the way in which two variables are associated. It can be 1:1 – the longer the forearm, the longer the total arm – or it can show deviations. For example, the larger a mammal is, the more of its body consists of bone. Why? Because the strength of bone only goes up as the square of bone width, whereas body weight goes up as the cube. Thus larger bodies, weighing more, require relatively more bone. But what about antler size, I wanted to know. Why is it that the larger the body size of the deer, the *relatively* larger his antlers? Why would natural selection favor that?

Gould leaned back in his chair. No, you have this all wrong, he said. This is an *alternative* to natural selection, not a cause of natural selection. My head spun. Natural selection was unable to change a simple allometric relationship regarding antler size that it had presumably created in the first place? Had it not already done so in adjusting bone size to body size? As I left his office, I said to myself, "This fool thinks he is bigger than natural selection." Perhaps I should have more accurately said, "Bigger than Darwin," but I felt it as bigger than natural selection itself – surely Stephen was going for the gold.

Many of us theoretical biologists who knew Stephen personally thought he was something of an intellectual fraud precisely because he had a talent for coining terms that promised more than they could deliver, while claiming exactly the opposite. One example was the notion of "punctuated equilibria" – which simply asserted that rates of (morphological) evolution were not constant, but varied over time, often with periods of long stasis interspersed with periods of rapid change. All of this was well known from the time of Darwin. The classic example was bats. They apparently evolved very quickly from small non-flying mammals (in perhaps less than twenty million years) then stayed relatively unchanged once they reached the bat phenotype we are all familiar with today about fifty million years ago. Nothing very surprising here. Intermediate forms were apt to be neither very good classic mammals, nor good flying ones either, so natural selection pushed them rapidly through the relevant evolutionary space.

But Steve wanted to turn this into something grander, a justification for replacing natural selection (favoring individual reproductive success) with something called species selection. Since one could easily imagine that there was rapid turnover of species during periods of intense selection and morphological change, one might expect species selection to be more intense while during the rest of the equilibrium stabilizing selection would rule throughout. But the rate of species turnover has nothing to do with the traits within species, only with the relative frequency of species showing these traits. As would prove usual, Steve missed the larger interesting science by embracing a self-serving fantasy. Species selection today is a small but interesting topic in evolutionary theory, not some grand principle emerging from paleontological patterns.

Recently something brand new has emerged about Steve that is astonishing. In his empirical work attacking others for biased data analysis in the service of political ideology, it he who was guilty of bias in the service of his own political ideology. What is worse – and more shocking – is that Steve's errors seem to be extensive and the bias serious. A careful reanalysis of one case shows that his target is unblemished while his own attack is biased in all the ways Gould attributes to his victim. His most celebrated book (*The Mismeasure of Man*) starts with a takedown of Samuel George Morton. Morton was a scientist in the early 19th Century who devoted himself to measuring the human cranium, especially the volume of the inside, a rough estimate of the size of the enclosed brain. He did so meticulously by pouring first seeds and later ball bearings into skulls until they were full and then pouring them out and measuring their volume in a graduated cylinder. He was a pure empiricist. He knew brain size was an important variable, but very little about the details. (Indeed, we do not know much more today.) He thought his data would bear on whether we were one species or several, and they certainly bore out his racist preconceptions, upon which he was only too happy to elaborate. But still, he appeared to be creating a vast trove of true and useful facts.

I love these empiricists. They work for the future and gather data whose logic later generations will reveal. Precisely because they have no axes to grind or hypotheses to prove, their data are apt to be more reliable than the first wave after a new theory. I have benefitted from them in my own life, most memorably when I was shown a large and accurate literature on ratios of investment in twenty ant species, gathered long before anyone appreciated why these facts might be of some considerable interest, as indeed they were.

In any case, Morton grouped his data by population according to best estimates of gross relatedness, Amerindians with Amerindians, Africans with Africans, Nordic Europeans with Nordic, and so on. It is here, Gould alleged, that all sorts of errors were made that supported preconceived notions that among the people with smaller cranial capacity (and therefore stupider) would be Amerindians and Africans. For example, Gould claimed that Morton made more subgroups among Nordic people than tropical ones, thus permitting more of them to be above norm. But, in fact, the opposite was true. Morton reported more Amerindian subsamples than European, and routinely pointed out when particular Amerindian subsamples were as high or higher than the European mean, facts that Gould claimed Morton hid.

There is an additional contrast between Morton and Gould worth noting. To conjure up Morton's mistakes, Gould lovingly describes the action of unconscious bias at work: "Morton, measuring by seed, picks up a threateningly large Black skull, fills it lightly and gives a few desultory shakes. Next, he takes a distressingly small Caucasian skull, shakes hard, and pushes mightily at the foramen magnum with his thumb. It is easily done, without conscious motivation; expectation is a powerful guide to action." Indeed it is, but careful re-measures show that Morton never made this particular mistake. Only three skulls were mismeasured as being larger than they were and these were all either Amerindian or African.

The same can't be said of Gould. He came across distressingly objective data collected by Morton, and by introducing biased procedures (no sample size below four) he was able to get appropriately biased results. And by misrepresenting the frequency of Nordic versus Amerindian subpopulations, he was able to create an illusion of bias where none existed, by mere emphatic assertion (no one bothered to check).

Where are the unconscious processes at work here? Is Steve flying upside-down on auto-pilot, unconsciously making the choices (substitute Nordic for Tropical, delete all samples smaller than four) that will invite the results he wants while hiding his bias? Is the conscious organism really completely in the dark while all of this is going on? Hard to imagine. But at the end, the organism appears to be in full self-deception mode: a blow-hard fraudulently imputing fraud, with righteous indignation, coupled with magnanimous forgiveness for the frailties of self-deception in others.

In response to this criticism, which was first brought to light by Lewis et al, the keeper of Gould's Tomb, his longtime editor at Natural History, Richard Milner, had some choice comments in Stephen's defense. Gould, he said, "was a tireless crusader against racism in any form." (That is, with full self-deception.) He also said that any bias was, "On the side of the angels." But who of us is in any position to say what is on the side of the angels? We barely know what's in our own self-interest. And getting around these problems is the whole point of the scientific method.

A general point is that it is often very hard to draw the line between conscious and unconscious deception – or to define the precise mixture of the two. Linguistic analysis in 2010, for instance, suggested that the architects of the 2003 U.S. war on Iraq were speaking deceptively when they warned that Saddam Hussein had caused 9/11 and Iraq possessed WMDs. I naively thought that this analysis showed conscious deception (Trivers 2011) but I no longer agree with myself. Unconscious deception could cause the same symptoms – reduced use of the words "I" and "we," fewer qualifiers, and so on.

GEORGE C. WILLIAMS

I never spotted a drop of deceit and self-deception in George Williams. He was as straight and true as he was tall. The last time I spoke with him was in 2002 when I called about something and he told me he had pre-Alzheimer's. There were simple memory tests now that were diagnostic, he said. In the background I could hear his wife Doris saying something. George said, "Doris always tells me not to tell people," and continued by saying that what he first noticed was that all words starting with capital letters were disappearing from his mind – arbitrary words for cities, buildings, people, and so on.

A few months later, I sent my *Selected Papers* book to him but I never heard back. He was gone. The person I felt for was Doris, a beautiful woman about half his size, and a very welcome complement to him. It's those closest to someone with Alzheimer's who often suffer the most, but George had a sweet disposition that, I hear, greatly reduced the cost to those closest to him.

We last saw each other when we were at the William Hamilton memorial session at Amherst in 2000 during the meetings of the Human Behavior and Evolution Society. Both of us were slated to speak. He was sitting behind me while Richard Dawkins was talking, and I could hear Doris saying, "Now, George, don't do what you are thinking of. Just tell the stories you have about Bill. Don't do it." So I was full of anticipation when George got up because I knew he was surely going to do exactly what his wife thought was a bad idea. Sure enough, George got up and said, "I wish Bill were here today because I have a bone to pick with him."

He then proceeded to pick that bone for the entire talk. It had to do with the evolution of sex and patterns of evidence that George had pointed out years ago that contradicted (so George said) aspects of Bill's parasite approach. I thought it was wonderful. There were those who said that his talk was inappropriate, and why didn't he just tell stories. But I thought it was perfect for the occasion. Both vintage George Williams – no wasted motion with that organism! – and a tribute to the enduring importance of Bill's ideas.

My first contact with George was when I was a graduate student. I sent him my chapter then in press on parental investment and sexual selection. When I wrote the paper I had completely forgotten that a key portion of the argumentation came right out of George's 1966 book, *Adaptation and Natural Selection*. I had only relearned this when I reread his book in preparation for teaching my first course on social evolution. There were "sex role reversed" species in his book (as well as female choice for genes and investment) and the relevant pages were full of underlining and marginal comments by me. None of this was acknowledged in the chapter I was sending him, so I pointed this out and said I would try to put some in before the book was printed. I was therefore feeling a little nervous when a letter came from George Williams. I braced myself for an unpleasant experience.

Instead, I found one of the warmest and most generous letters I have ever received. Among other things, he said my paper had rendered obsolete a chapter in his own forthcoming book *Sex and Evolution*, namely the chapter on differential mortality by sex, which chapter he enclosed. He said nothing about not being properly cited but dealt only with scientific content. His chapter had my essential insight regarding male mortality – that higher variance in male reproductive success would often select for traits more costly in survival. The larger book was the first to systematically explore the consequences of seeing that sex usually has an immediate fifty-percent cost in every generation (compared to asexuality), which cost has to be overcome in any successful model.

I invited him to Harvard in 1974 and he lectured on his ideas on sex. I do not say he was shy so much as reserved, but with a warm smile and sense of humor. My favorite joke of his occurred when George was telling me about the joys of grandfatherhood. "If I could have figured out how to have grandchildren without having children first, I would have done so." Later on, I knew just what he meant – high relatedness, no work. Or as Melvin Newton (Huey's brother) once put it, "You can serve them ice cream for breakfast, what do you care?"

Having started with the evolution of senescence in 1957, in later life George tackled Darwinian Medicine, memorably saying that he did not think there was any compound, arsenic included, that was not beneficial if given in sufficiently small doses. This was almost surely an overstatement, but a bracing and useful one. His knowledge of biology was so deep that he is the only person I know of to have predicted in advance the existence of an entire category of selfish genetic elements (genes that spread within an individual because they are advantageous to themselves, not the individual). Called 'androgenesis' it occurs when paternal genes eject maternal ones and take over the genome of an organism, a system now known from three very different groups of organisms.

He was a beautiful man, with a very simple and clear style of thinking and a warm and humble personality. He was especially good at seeing through gibberish, whether it was group selection or psychoanalysis – and advancing carefully and slowly on major issues.

CHAPTER 14

Ambivalence About Jamaica

I have spent perhaps eighteen years of my life in Jamaica. I own a home and property there in the most rural parish, full of mango trees, guava, coconut, and every kind of citrus, not to mention insects, birds, and lizards. I married onto the island. I have spent eight years there on research, mostly studying lizards but also degree of bodily symmetry in our own species. I have five Jamaican-American children, including twin girls, all blessedly living in the U.S. along with their mothers and my nine grandchildren.

Upon arrival I loved the sexual freedom of Jamaica, the wonderful sense of humor, and also the freedom I felt from the U.S. past. Slavery and post-slavery were never as bitter in Jamaica as in the U.S. because the slaves and later dark-skinned Jamaicans greatly outnumbered the whites and the browns. Furthermore, it was not *my* problem. None of my ancestors had anything to do with Jamaica, and while both my parents were solid anti-racists still I felt the guilt in the U.S. of being a white man indirectly benefitting from a racist system. In Jamaica, I felt free and one step above a tourist. I was a scientist, actually working on the island to contribute knowledge about the island. Furthermore, in the countryside I enjoyed a kind of protection that would later evaporate. If a Jamaican jumped on me, chances are six Jamaicans would jump on him – "wha you attack the foreigner for, the tourist him?"

I still love all these things about the island, especially the humor, but over the past forty-five years I have come to see a good deal of ugliness in this beautiful place. The murder rate has increased tenfold and is now island-wide. Only a handful of countries have higher murder rates. At this point nine-ty-five percent of tourists stay at all-inclusive hotels, known in Jamaica as "all-exclusives" – they must be paid for in advance and you cannot enter from the outside without buying an expensive pass. This has made the rest of the country even more dangerous, and gun crime has spread to every parish. In the Black River area, you can rent a gun for two weeks. But make sure you return it on time. If not, when they come for the gun they'll come for you too.

The sexual ignorance in Jamaica is strong, to put it mildly, and one effect is violence against those known (through self-admission, for example) or suspected of being homosexual. Six months after I arrived in 1968 a man was stoned to death after being seen fornicating with another man. Forty years later they are still stoning and murdering people for suspected homosexuality. In early 2015 an effeminate youth in Montego Bay was tied to a tree with wire and rope and then stoned to death while the mob chanted, "Death to the botty bwoy." He was finally killed when a rock split his skull in two. It's on YouTube but I have not had the heart to watch it. Decent Jamaican friends of mine denied the crime, as they almost always do – "I hear he was really a thief and they caught him stealing." But they don't tie up a thief with wire and taunt him sexually, they hold him down, call him a "dutty tief," and beat him.

A Jamaican Doctorate in Law from Oxford, a Jamaican woman of high intelligence and class, loves Buju Banton's music and says she hears Buju was entrapped by the FBI for his anti-homosexuality. Must be the first time in U.S. history, I thought. I had just told her that Buju was a fool, and I had no sympathy for him. He was caught in an FBI sting operation on a cocaine deal. He could have pled guilty as did the other guilty parties – caught on film and tape – and received a five-year sentence. Instead he chose to fight it, partly on the notion that the homosexual lobby was behind this FBI operation (what they were behind was a publicity campaign in the U.S. attacking his music) – and he got ten years. I doubt the FBI was unhappy when he pled "not guilty." Here were the lyrics he sang to audiences of tens of thousands in Jamaica and abroad. "Boom-bye-bye-in-a-botty-bwoy head," and "Everytime me see a botty bwoy, him haf feh dead." The man is publicly advocating murder on a mass scale to large crowds of people. He got off light.

I have grown increasingly ambivalent about Jamaica. The physical beauty is overwhelming, the women gorgeous, willing, and plentiful. But, as Jamaicans say, "Jamaica would be a beautiful island except for we Jamaicans," by which they suggest mostly the men.

G SPENDS SEVEN YEARS IN PRISON FOR A CRIME HE DID NOT COMMIT

I first began to develop a deep distaste for Jamaica in general, and Southfield in particular, about ten years after I joined the community. By that time, I had married into it, received land as a gift, and built both a small farmhouse and an enjoining water-tank. Daytimes I spent on my property allegedly working on social theory based on natural selection but in fact consuming much more THC than was consistent with forward progress on any subject. I slept down the road at my mother-in-law's at night, with my wife and our child, so my house was available at night for occupancy.

One day Be-be came to me and said that G, a fellow smoker at our camp, had nowhere to sleep since his mother had asked him to move out of her home. He had been living in a closet but then she repainted the closet and this apparently raised its value above G's, so G had to go. G was short for GP, which was short for General Penitentiary, which is where he had spent the last seven years of a ten-year sentence for a minor crime he hadn't committed. He'd only recently been released.

What made G's case particularly galling was that not only hadn't he committed the crime, but he couldn't have and everyone knew it. He was accused of beating up a shopkeeper, but at the time the crime was being committed he'd been at his job, cleaning up after one of the local weekly film showings. Not only that, but G was small and slim, incapable of inflicting the damage the shopkeeper sustained. The shopkeeper knew it wasn't G who'd beaten him up. In fact, he and most other people knew it was a gangster youth who later spent fifteen years in prison for murder and ended up committing suicide.

But G was made to take the fall. Why was never clear to me except that G did have the habit of preachifying and condemning, Rasta-style, the wicked, the covetous, and the deceitful. Among those he preached against was this particular shopkeeper. That may have been the reason it was pinned on him. But what sealed his fate was his very low status in the community's hierarchy. G was poor. G was small. G had no powerful relatives. The economic elite had decided he was going to prison, and everyone else fell in line.

G's boss could easily have vouched for his alibi, but he happened to be the brother of the shopkeeper. There had been twenty other people at the film-showing, and each of them knew where G was when the assault took place. Not a single one spoke up for him. His own people had money for neither bail nor an attorney, and apparently G lacked any more powerful friend willing to take up his cause. I was told that when G heard his ten-year sentence handed down in Black River Court, a single tear rolled down his face.

His first several months in prison, G was beaten mercilessly because the shopkeeper paid warders for this extra work. What G suffered at the hands of his fellow prisoners I never asked. I did ask him once if he ever managed to get ganja in prison, and he replied that without ganja he would not have survived. Why? Because he became one of the men who caught the ganja thrown over the wall and dealt it to other prisoners. I'm sure almost all the proceeds went to others, but at least he had a highly valued job within the system.

Then an extraordinary thing happened. G had been living on my property for several years well-treated when I left for four months and returned to discover that the community that had allowed him to go to prison for no crime at all except being poor and slim, had now joined together to attack him on three separate occasions.

First, a well-known thug held him down on the road late at night and threatened to kill him because, "The white man land a fe me" – meaning my land was for him because his father had planted some willow trees for me – and then failed to care for them by letting tall grass grow up around them. (He was the first to teach me that trees can actually shrink in size.) What made this attack particularly threatening was that this particular thug worked as a side-man on a mini-bus that left Southfield for Kingston six times a

GE-GO ON THE BACK PORCH. Seven years in prison for nothing at all. (Photo courtesy Robert Trivers.)

week, making him the perfect figure to point out a victim to be shot during a "robbery" along the route.

The second attack on G came from a super-size Jamaican woman, perhaps five-foot-ten-inches tall, and at least 260 pounds. She'd grabbed and man-handled him outside her home on the road, claiming that G had told her boyfriend about her other lovers (an unlikely claim).

Finally, G was set upon by a group at a local bar after he drove up on his brand new ride, an $800 Japanese bicycle with fifteen speeds that I had im-ported for him on my last visit. Apparently he'd come through saying, "The Japanese a come through," and this set off the crowd.

When I learned about these attacks on G, I went on a two-day tear. I first went to the yard of the side-man, but he ran out back as I came in yelling for him. I stayed up all night with a friend, and at six a.m. I appeared where the bus picked him up. I held my fist to his jaw, an upper cut ready, and said,

"Ge-go is fe *me*! He is *mine* and anybody harm him must deal with *me*."
He seemed to get the idea. Indeed, from then on G rode the bus free. I also
cursed out the large woman from the road, careful not to step an inch onto
her property, and received verbal abuse in return. Perhaps she got the idea and
perhaps not. I know the shopkeeper did because I went in and asked him in
a loud voice if I was safe in his shop, since I knew G was not. I then jumped
the counter.

G finally died of spinal meningitis, a disease he most likely contracted in
prison.

JAMAICAN HOMOPHOBIA

My relationship with Jamaica has not been helped by its rabid homophobia.
I have been all over the world and have never seen levels of homophobia as
high as in Jamaica. It does no good to tell Jamaicans that the scientific evidence is clear that the most anti-homosexual men are precisely those with
the greatest latent homosexual content to their make-up.

Part of the problem is the Jamaican retention of the British anti-sodomy
laws, making it a crime worth twelve years in prison. Amazing, isn't it? A
bunch of upper-class Brits, probably of dubious sexuality themselves, hand
down laws making everyone else highly vulnerable to prosecution for an activity they surely engaged in sometimes safely in private among themselves.
In the UK these laws were successively abolished from 1967 to 1981, but in
Jamaica they live on. Whenever someone is attacked for actual or suspected
homosexuality, the police typically hide behind the "anti sodomy" laws. They
justify their lack of protection for homosexual men by pointing out that such
men are all but self-admitted felons, only awaiting observational data to put
them away for twelve years. But it must be admitted that three years ago a
police officer in Mandeville intervened in a mob attack on a small house in
which two men lived together. The intended victims were not killed, but the
policeman had to run for his life and go into hiding because he was now a
marked man.

Jamaicans are proud to be Jamaican and proud to be proud, but how is keeping laws that make simple sexual acts into twelve-year felonies a matter of national pride when the colonial masters who introduced these laws have now abolished them at home? Apparently, Jamaica is trying to be the England of five hundred years ago, at least sexually.

Another part of the problem may be that so many boys are raised only by a mother. Certainly in the rural countryside women in their twenties are often not living with the biological father of one or more children. Men are often not invested in their own children but instead use their money to support their current lover(s) and her children. Since they have no fathers, boys may lack a paternal model. They may also express a deep ambivalence toward their mother. One parent must embody both the warm loving figure, the single parent they have, but also the harsh disciplinary figure (a role in my life played by my father). What kinds of internal sexual identities problem are bred in this system, who knows?

In response to this non-action by police I have recently joined with twelve other men to create the Homosexual Defense League, based on the Panther credo that if no one else will protect you we will try. If that requires putting the fear of God into some people all the better. If you are going to run a sexually ignorant and abusive island where innocent people are publicly tortured and stoned, expect a few people to stand up and try to put an end to it.

We are all of us in the League heterosexual men, but we have agreed to prevent these kinds of atrocities whenever we can. Right now we only operate in Southeast St. Elizabeth, but I hope it spreads to other areas. So far I have had no problem signing up volunteers to tip us off when our services might be needed. On a given night, you may receive a call at four in the morning telling you it would be helpful if you were at so-and-so a place. I'm willing to put my life on the line when those calls come. We will roll in to protect life and if we are late we will gather evidence. We will not just "stand around and look."

JAMAICAN MISOGYNY

But the sexual ignorance of Jamaican men goes way beyond their legendary homophobia. It is widely believed, for instance, that kissing a woman's pum-pum just before giving her the ghetto slam is itself homosexual. The very phrase "bow cat man" suggests a connection, since as you lower yourself to kiss the blessed structure, you elevate your rear-end. All of this foolishness is, of course, strictly beneficial to me. Men so ignorant as not to know how to please a woman sexually? Sure does open up opportunities.

Or here's another colorful example: the most severe insult between adult Jamaican men is, "You are a sanitary napkin." (The phrase also happens to be an offense against the law; a forty-shilling word under the British.) I almost fell to the ground when I first learned in Kingston what these big, muscular men were yelling at each other with ascending volume: from ras-klat (ass cloth) to bomba-clot (slang for pum-pum) to p...sy clot (close) to blood clot (the real red thing). I resolved, absent imminent threat, never to fear these men again.

When an American man calls you a "mother fucker" he is at least making an assertion about your moral character – you are the kind of man who would force sex on his own mother. What are you alleging when you call someone a "ras-clot," though? I think it must be that you are the least valuable woman imaginable, one who is both reproductively and sexually unavailable and is excreting what are often imagined to be poisons or germs – no, just her previous month's investment in possible procreation. I was once told that the expression originated in whorehouses, where the "ras clot man" was the one whose duty it was to collect together the used sanitary napkins and dispose of them. But it is hard to imagine that the island was so saturated with whorehouses that a universal term of abuse would spring from them alone. There must be some psychological connection between calling other men "used sanitary napkins" and murdering them if they are suspected of having sex with each other, but I can't see it.

SURVIVING AN ARMED HOME INVASION ROBBERY

The low point in my relationship with Jamaica came fairly recently.

In 2007 I won the Crafoord Prize from the Swedish Royal Society. It was worth $500,000. When it was announced in the local Jamaican newspaper, I knew immediately that I had a brand new problem on the island. Although the paper had gotten most of the details wrong, including having me as a Jamaican who had migrated to the U.S. to study lizards, it got the sum of money I had been awarded correct. Most people downgraded it in their mind to US$5000 or its Jamaican equivalent, US$10,000, but even this was a large enough sum that, were I stupid enough to store it at home, my place would be well worth robbing.

Sure enough, in the spring of 2008 I returned to my home from a local bar to a most unwelcome experience. It was ten thirty at night. Luckily, I had been in the bar with my computer, working on my self-deception book (*Folly of Fools*) because I preferred writing surrounded by company to writing alone. This meant that I had only been smoking and drinking very modestly, and this may have helped saved my life.

I unlocked the door to my bedroom, turned on the lights, opened the windows for fresh air, and left the bedroom door wide open as usual. Still feeling strong of mind and body, I decided to pack for my trip to Montego Bay the next day. I was supposed to fly out of the country early the following morning, and if I pack the day before I still have the chance to remember what I've forgotten before it's too late. Suddenly I had the uncomfortable feeling that I was not alone in my bedroom. I turned and saw two ugly young dark-skinned men in their twenties just inside the room. My thoughts must have raced because I remember thinking very quickly – where am I? In China? In some warp in the space-time continuum? No. Had I forgotten an appointment, as I often do? No – since when was I meeting with two butt-ugly young men in my bedroom at ten thirty at night?

Then I saw that one had a machete and the other a long knife. Ah ohh, I said to myself, bending back slightly – I know what this is, this is an armed robbery. Simultaneously I drew a long straight strong encased Brazilian six-inch blade knife from the right side of my pants, blade pointed toward the right testicle. As they spotted my knife their faces went from terror-inducing to terror-expressing, and they just managed to escape my room before I could corner either. In fact, I went straight at the cutlass man since he was the more vulnerable, within two feet of him he could do no more than slap me on my back, while I could slash him to death. The other was more "problematic."

I had never thought about this possibility in more than fifteen years living there. My house lay at the end of a long dirt driveway off of a one-way lane to the main road, some half a kilometer below. Since, as it turned out, they were both local boys, it hardly seemed credible (in retrospect) that I was meant to survive the robbery. They could not say, "Well, den, Marse Bob, see you in the square tomorrow." Also it is a well-known fact of human psychology that the longer someone holds you under control, the crueler they become and the likelier to indulge in "the final solution." I always tell people, especially women under sexual attack, counter-attack at once and make a big noise to attract people – do not submit, and for God's sake do not be taken captive. Attack and scream to draw people, otherwise matters only get worse. Begging for mercy often merely excites the aggression it seeks to avert.

Once they scurried out the front door, I locked it behind them. Then the true terror began. Since I had not come running out with a gun to blast a few shots at them, they surmised correctly that I was unarmed. It also turned out that I only had the knife because someone had very foolishly locked my personal fighting machete into the tool shed out back. Now the men wanted to re-enter the house. They began with soft knocking and absurd entreaties such as, "Let us in, we are the police."

Now I panicked. I had a huge one-floor house with numerous jalousie windows that could easily be entered by removing or smashing the glass panels. Then it would be two against one – as it was before – but without any element of surprise from me. That I had dozens of empty wine bottles escaped my notice entirely. Each was more dangerous than a knife, and in combination, throwing some broken bottles at close quarters and lunging with others, one could counter a machete. Having never envisioned this situation I had never planned for it, and that was a critical failing on my part.

I then made a most unwise decision. I abandoned my house in order to run out back and head down a hill full of old trees and bushes, nearly impenetrable and completely safe – if I could reach it. Alas, the boys were on that side of the house. I'll never forget the sight of a machete held high, gleaming in the moonlight as they took off after me. I slipped and fell but my Filipino martial arts teachers (Arnis) had taught me what to do in that situation: I was to pretend I was riding a bicycle upside-down, while flashing my blade in every direction. The kicking feet divert your attacker while you attack.

Sure enough, it worked. I put my knife through the calf of the taller thief, who had landed closer to me than was wise, while I cut the shorter one across his throat as he leaned over to attack me – alas not deeply enough to kill him. Both ran off, and I returned to my house. But I was so terrified that I couldn't be certain if they had run away, as they had, or were lurking around for a second attack.

I had called the police early on, and they had promised to send a car. It was a scant ten-minute drive from the police station to my house, but it took them a full hour to reach my yard. When they finally did, they kept quiet at the edge until I came out on the porch at which point they apparently decided it was safe to enter because they turned on their police lights and approached.

One officer stayed in the vehicle the entire time, while the other one wanted to search my home on the basis of the blood trail leading out of it. I pointed out that the blood came from my own wound (wounded by myself as I thrashed my knife around upside down) so it merely tracked my movements. But I couldn't deter him from entering my home. I at least prevented him from entering my bedroom, which he was eager to do.

At no time did he search the outside premises, ask to see where the near-fatal encounter had occurred – where we would have found a slipper that I found in the morning, which indicated the youths came from nearby – nor did he walk around the house and notice the broken bathroom window where they were preparing to enter right before I rushed out. The police drove off, and that was it.

I spent the night at a friend's home. Mr. Cameron was a school principal with whom I had worked for many years. He had a licensed gun, and his wife tended to my wound, but I was well frightened by then and no amount of safety felt like enough. Later, I was to marvel that I'd never thought to call Mr. Cameron while the incident was unfolding – far closer than the police, far more in the know, and far more on my side. That kind of blindness can kill you, but luckily, in this case, it didn't.

My assailants were arrested, but after the arrests the detective called to say that I owed him a computer in payment. I got "rahtid," as we say in Jamaica – extremely angry. If the thieves don't get your money, the police will. I told him not to raise the issue with me again. He said it was for his daughter. I again told him not to raise the subject with me. So he sold the case out on the bottom side. The employer and pastor of one of the men and a friend of the other put together the $500 necessary to buy off two five-year prison felonies. When they were brought on for trial they looked around scared and asked, "Did the white man come?" The detective said no. He had in fact deprived me of the right to testify by never informing me of the court date. The charge was downgraded to a $130 fine for robbing a man in the public square by threatening him with a machete.

The other day I met a Jamaican of around my age who had just sold his home and a second house he owned in Ft. Lauderdale in order to retire to Jamaica. Ahh, I said, you are finally enjoying your dream of retiring to Jamaica! "No," he said, "I'm leaving this coming Thursday to return to Ft. Lauderdale. Here is way too dangerous." After dark, he said, even when it was his wife or daughter knocking to ask entrance, he could never be sure there wasn't a man there too, holding a gun to her head as she was requesting entry.

Nobody is running me out of Jamaica – as Huey Newton's father put it, you have to take a killing but you don't have to take a beating. I have not yet taken a beating and hope I never will. As for a killing, I am seventy-two years old. If it comes, it comes. It would certainly cost me less in lost years than a lot of others I've known and continue to mourn, men like Be-be and G and Peter Tosh, women like Celestine, and many, many others.

JAMAICAN HUMOR

And yet, for all my hatred of Jamaica's culture of violence and sexual ignorance, its lawlessness and cruelty, it is still my adopted home. So let me end this chapter by describing one of Jamaica's most attractive features: its sense of humor.

From the moment I arrived in Jamaica I have enjoyed its particular brand of verbal comedy, which is often sexual in tone and frequently involves deception. Indeed, it was through Jamaican humor that I first saw that deception was more common in the tropics, as others have noted, as well as being treated there with less moralistic anger and more humor – at least most of the time.

Jamaican phrases are particularly rife with this sort of humor. "Finger-fere" is to interfere by pilfering or rearranging objects with your fingers. To make a "beefsteak" is to make a mistake in your own favor. A trivial example would be a shopkeeper giving you change biased in his favor. He has made a mistake, but since he has benefitted from it he has actually made a beefsteak. Or another classic – if you are heard complimenting yourself people like to say, "Self-praise is no recommendation."

The new phrase for having your institutions rob from you is, "Hol' down, tek weh" – as when my bank tells me it will take them thirty working days (six weeks) to clear a check I give them on my account back in the U.S. The reverse takes at most four days, and typically you get the full deposit one day after it hits your account. What do they do down here? They take your money and invest it for five weeks, remove the profits, and give you back your money. Hol' down, tek weh.

Jamaica is an incredibly corrupt and thieving country, top to bottom. It ranks far down the list of corrupt countries with ten years of negligible economic growth to show for it. The joke for how it works at all levels is "hol down, tek weh." The other day the Prime Minister, Portia Simpson, asked for one hundred percent forgiveness of IMF debt, not eighty, not ninety-five, but the full one hundred. The loan itself had had no positive economic impact whatsoever on the county as a whole. The money was merely bled off from the top, in that the higher up you were the more you got of it. Hol' down, tek weh.

My personal favorite Jamaican linguistic innovation is the cluster of phrases that arise out of the term "to give a man a jacket" for fathering another man's child. The degree to which the jacket fits is critical. Thus to cut a man a "waistcoat" is to give him a jacket (child) so perfectly resembling him as to require no additional tailoring. As the Senegalese put the same problem, better to have an ugly child who resembles you than a good-looking one who resembles your neighbor.

Here is a typical Jamaican humorous exchange:

"Ralph, how long you been married?"

"Thirty years."

"Do you still love your wife as much as you did the day you married her?"

"The way I see it, you stick with the evil you know."

Bob Marley puts the more general problem as follows: "The truth is, everyone is going to hurt you. You just got to find the ones worth suffering for."

To finish off this chapter on Jamaica, let me relate two extended jokes that were made to me that I regard as vintage Jamaican.

Once, I was returning from the Blue Mountains north of Kingston with three lizard workers. At 8:30 p.m. we came to the fish market by roadside in Old Harbor, where women sat with big pans of fried fish between their legs, skirts tucked in. Since this was the last place that sold food for the rest of our three-hour journey, I pulled in. Three women jumped up with trays of fried fish and ran toward me, knowing that I was underwriting this enterprise. I told them I did not eat fish, and they should go to the other men. Two ran off toward my workers, but one stayed back. She was short and stocky, maybe 240 pounds and fifty years old; nothing soft about her. As we walked toward the others, she said, "You don't eat fish, but I bet you eat fishy." (Pum-pum.) I said, "Yes nuh man, do you know where I can buy any?" "Right ya so, right ya so," she said, flashing two fingers between her legs, and we shared a jovial laugh between us - but nothing more.

The other joke stems from an unlikely source, an alleged rape. Miss Cassy was a famous beauty in Southfield – tall; elegant; wonderful, long face. I never actually laid eyes on her because by the time I arrived she was in her early seventies and too sick to come outside. Instead you would only see her on her porch, in her nightclothes, cutting a tall and elegant figure in the distance. Finally, even that was too much for her, and she was bedridden.

One day, the rumor spread that Miss Cassy had been raped. A strong forty-five-year-old man had been pulled off her and the cry went out around the town. The rapist was Miss Cassy's son-in-law, married to her daughter – a woman notably less attractive than her mother.

The man was held while the police were called from the distant station of Bull Savannah. It took the police about two hours to arrive. When they did, they found the rapist held by several men on the verandah while Miss Cassy was inside. One officer had the bright idea of checking on Miss Cassy and went inside to ask her if she had been raped. She replied, "Him deya all the while." Meaning this affair had been going on for some time, presumably unnoticed by others.

This had three immediate effects. The man was set free, his captors slunk off in embarrassment and shame, and the police left thoroughly disappointed that they had no rapist to molest that night. And then, within minutes, a fourth effect: an expression was shooting around the community that endures to this very day – "Him deya all the while."

For weeks and weeks people convulsed with laughter whenever it was uttered. I never heard what happened with the alleged rapist – how exactly did he deal with his wife? – but forty-five years later, a lizard worker of mine commented on the fact that a certain young adult male green lizard always appeared at the same time of day, at the same spot, during our observations by noting, "Him deya all the while." The rest of us had a good laugh, old enough to remember the original joke, a meme propagating itself now for more than forty-five years. It's hard not to love a place at least a little when you know forty-five years worth of its jokes.

CHAPTER 15

Looking Back and Looking Forward

I am seventy-two years old now, having devoted fifty years to the study of evolutionary biology, a combination of social theory based on natural selection wedded to genetics – the very backbone of all of life. I have had the good fortune to help lay the foundation for a variety of flourishing sub-disciplines, from reciprocal altruism and parent-offspring conflict to within-individual genetic conflict and self-deception. Through this work, I have met many extraordinary individuals, several of whom were my teachers. I have also gotten to know up close and personal many non-human animals. I have "enjoyed" an unusual number of near-death experiences – due in part to my tendency toward intense interpersonal disagreements late at night.

Yet when I look back on this show, there is one thing I regret and it is absence of self-reflection. Yes I would live life and study it, but would I study my own life? Time and time again, the answer comes back "no." Yet exactly whose life is the more important to you: others or your own? "You self-deceptionist," my first wife would sneer. "You talk a lot about parent-offspring conflict, yet you neglect your own son." Guilty as charged. Too much ambition and too little thought about my family: wife, children, and myself.

Major decisions, such as where to go when I decided to leave Harvard in 1978, were made without any serious thought at all – how about a name professorship at the University of New Mexico or a major offer from the University of Rochester with its powerful biology department? These were brushed aside with scarcely a glance. Instead I simply trotted off to the University of California at Santa Cruz because my wife and I had enjoyed a pleasant weekend with Burney LeBoeuf, his wife, and his elephant seals. I even remember mumbling to myself at one point, "Oh, we'll let auto-pilot handle this or that problem." Autopilot? As a means of choosing which of three universities and cities you should live in for the next fifteen years? By definition autopilot is the opposite of careful conscious introspection and evaluation – it is what you do when the path forward is obvious and no rational reflection is needed.

Consider one little fact I did not know. The Atlantic Ocean arrives from the tropics on the East Coast, so that it is warm enough to swim in during the summer near Boston, but the Pacific Ocean comes from the Arctic. You have to reach almost as far south as Los Angeles before it is warm enough to swim. I easily imagined many happy summers in Santa Cruz swimming with my young children in this seaside town. Instead I remember vividly painful days our first summer there, with me and my children plastered to the sand in the sun, so cold was the water that it made the surrounding air too cold to bear. It was only I that braved the water itself, dashing in, dunking myself and dashing right back out. I had learned to swim in the cool waters of Denmark yet could not stand more than a quick in and out. In Santa Cruz my children could only briefly step into the water, so a third of the value of the place was a mirage. For seven years we hardly ever visited the ocean.

Good planning, Bob, makes the winter cold of Rochester seem much more tolerable, doesn't it? Especially when a close friend and great biologist (who had also entertained me and my wife warmly in his home) had been willing to create a major position. And what was the problem with New Mexico? I had spent a summer working in Albuquerque as a day laborer building their university's football stands. Were there too many Mexican-Americans for me to see an obvious place for us? But then why as a man married to a Jamaican woman would I choose a town with a one percent African-American population? Just because Huey Newton was waved in front of me as a graduate student at Santa Cruz? To me Santa Cruz was a disastrous sixteen-year choice, and I have a broken marriage, broken family, and record of non-productivity to prove it. Yes I did get to meet and befriend Huey Newton and enjoy being a Black Panther, doubtless with near-death experiences I knew nothing about. But could this repay the devastation on my life and that of my family – of inadequate pay, research support, colleagues, social environment, and personal productivity? Served me right: if you don't think through a problem, you shouldn't act surprised when later it looks as if no one has thought it through.

Santa Cruzians were so laid-back that when I returned from lecturing in the Midwest or the East Coast they often seemed to be sleepwalking, they moved so slowly. If you strung together three sentences in a logical order, a person might well hold up a hand and say, "Hey, wait a second, brother, back off a bit, you're invading my personal space." The classic joke about Northern Californians has a woman meeting a man at a bar. Woman says, "Your place or my place?" Man says, "Hey look, if this is going to be a hassle let's forget about it."

I can remember getting up to lecture to about eighty people at Harvard while I was still at Santa Cruz and realizing half way through the lecture that women back East were actually attracted to men with good minds. I had a chance there! Especially relevant to me now that my marriage was crumbling about me. I had no woman in Santa Cruz, no one short of Oakland, itself far away. There is no question that the people I would have been meeting in Rochester would resemble those in Boston much more than those at Santa Cruz.

There are other such major "decisions" I could name, and also plenty of occasions of unconsciousness or fear in which I failed to act by my own principles. Fortunately I remember only a small fraction of these, perhaps twenty in all. But each of them can bite hot to this day.

THE WAY FORWARD

What is the way forward? There is one obstacle and there is one hope. The obstacle is self-deception, which is a powerful force with immense repetitive power. The hope is that after becoming more deeply conscious of one's own self-deceptions and of the possible means of ameliorating them, one can make some real progress against this strong negative force. In recent years, I've been trying to do this more and more.

One of the few self-deceptions I've been able to reverse concerns the order in which I search for something lost. Consider two opposite strategies. On the first strategy, you first look where you most expect to find the missing item, then you move to the second most likely, then third, and down the line. This is the rational strategy; it maximizes chance of success while minimizing costs. Now imagine you do it the other way around. First you search where you least expect to find the item, then try the second least expected, and so on toward the most expected. For as long as I can remember, I have almost exclusively used this second strategy.

And yet for many years I was conscious that my strategy was counterintuitive without stopping to consider why I was doing it this way. Once I did, the answer was fairly obvious. My father used to punish me harshly whenever I failed to find something of his or of mine. That created a fear in me, and the least-likely-first strategy offered immediate psychological protection from mounting terror. If I looked in the likeliest place first and the item wasn't there, I'd be confronted with the realization that every choice thereafter was less likely than the one before. But when I adopted the reverse strategy and didn't find it where it was least likely to be the next spot could only be *more* hopeful. I could hold onto hope right up until the very end, at which point the missing item would either be there (relief) or not (terror - but at least deferred for as long as possible).

Since making this realization, I've forced myself to re-orient to the rational strategy even if my first impulse is still to start wrong. As soon as I begin searching in the unlikeliest of places, I seize myself and say, "No, let us go look where this is *most* likely to be found." This seems to work better more the more I practice it.

What about repetitive self-admiration? I have a repertoire of between sixty and eighty jokes spanning many years, personalities, and situations and honed over time from a larger sample. Told right, they almost invariably amuse the audience, including myself. But I sit there watching this show and saying, "Can't you shut the fuck up for a change? Do you really want to waste the next two minutes hearing this for the fiftieth time? Why not see if someone else has something interesting to say?" This is an easy behavior to change. Now when I start in on one of my oldies-but-goodies I can cut myself off and say to the other person: "Never mind that, what were you saying?"

A more costly form of self-deception involves my spiteful side. If you say something insulting, I want to strike right back. If I fail to because I am slow or inhibited, trust me that whenever the event recurs in my mind I will torture myself, sometimes for years, with the rant I should have delivered and may do so now at full volume alone in my apartment far away.

And yet very often a spiteful response is not the best one. It can easily generate spite in return, and down the staircase the two of you descend. Inside me there are two voices. One cries out, Bob, you have made this mistake 630 times in the past and regretted every single one. Why not forego it this time. Then comes a stronger voice, "No, Bob, *this* time is different," and there goes 631.

It was an eye-opener to me to discover recently the value of friends in breaking this cycle. I was telling a good friend about a nasty message I had gotten from a woman and my intended nasty response. He wanted to know why. Because, I said, she said this, that, and the third thing, and it hurt. That was the key. He was unmoved by this argument. He'd suffered none of my internal hurt and was indifferent to it. Only three things were relevant to him: her message, my possible response, and its likely consequences. The likeliest consequence would be that she would write back an even nastier note, and I would be further estranged for no good reason. Why would I want to do that? Why indeed. The Concorde Fallacy all over again – you owe it to your past spite, despite it being a sunk cost, to double-down. Better, of course, to do nothing.

I've also been making an effort to actually think through major decisions. When I have a decision of some importance to make, I force myself to stop, rest, maybe even lie down and meditate. Then I make lists, think, rest again. No more autopilot. No more saying, "Oh, doing my work is more important than such trivia." Out of such trivia life is made. Even if it's only for the last eight years of my life, I'm trying to skip this self-deception nonsense and live a more conscious life, a life where I study more carefully the actual life I'm living and hopefully enjoy the life more fully.

Naturally I plan to keep working. My Jamaican symmetry project is twenty years old, and we have now shown that knee symmetry is a key variable in sprinting success; we can use it to predict sprinting success fourteen years into the future, and also to predict which of Jamaica's elite sprinters are the very best. I will not found any new subdisciplines. My theoretical contributions will be more in the form of review articles. I am now trying to complete an article on species selection. No one has bothered, after all these years, to come up with a coherent account of the various conditions under which species prosper and generate new species, or fail and go extinct. This is in part because Stephen Gould expropriated the subject for his own uses and set back the development of a science by some twenty years. I am trying to help develop the underlying logic he failed to.

Near death experiences? We shall see. Recently two more of my dogs were poisoned, almost certainly by the same person who poisoned four earlier ones. What kind of behavior will be required to stop these illegal murders, all of which threaten my own security since the dogs are my first line of defense? Time will tell. Meanwhile, I have hardly mentioned personal reproduction at all in this book, yet I have five children and nine grandchildren, and they occupy an increasing fraction of my time. So there are perhaps two sources of joy in my life – my children and grandchildren and the continuing ability of science to generate new and exciting facts and vistas.

Regarding grandchildren I have reached the George Williams heaven of little or no investment paired with all the pleasure that comes from the company of a set of related, highly variable and energetic organisms, thriving because of the work of my own children, not me. And here I have noticed something brand new. It is not just that I am related to my children by half and hence expected to invest accordingly. The half relatedness also means relatively high genetic similarity. Over and over again I get a special pleasure from my children in shared jokes, shared ways of viewing things, shared logic, shared political views – much of whose 'share-dom' I think results from genetic similarity at the relevant loci. Of course we will have a high chance of enjoying the same jokes, aren't we fifty percent alike in the genes we are expected to vary in? For me I can no longer see the same pattern in my grandchildren, now only having a quarter chance of sharing the same genes. Plenty of genetic similarity but a greater amount of dissimilarity.

BURIAL PLANS

Bill Hamilton chose to describe his preferred burial and its aftermath in biologically vivid and poetic terms. He would die in the Brazilian rainforest, his body to be scavenged by burying beetles so that he could later fly out as a group of buzzing beetles, "Into the Brazilian wilderness between the stars." But this was not to be. He died in the UK and was buried in Wytham at Oxford. It took the love of the second half of his life, Luisa, to add the poetry of his vision, drawing on his bacterial/cloud/dispersal theory so that, "Eventually a drop of rain will join you to the flooded forest of the Amazon."

I am no W.D. and my burial plan is very simple. If you find me dead outside of Jamaica kindly cremate me – inexpensive and no place to point to. If in Jamaica, dig a circular hole beneath my favorite large pimento tree, three feet wide and at least ten feet deep, and drop me head-first into the hole. Throw in some dirt and call it a day – no plaques please. I will not become a bright buzzing burrowing beetle or bacterial cloud, just a few more pimento berries when in season. I add the details on positioning my body mostly to annoy my Jamaican friends. They think I should be resting comfortably on my side in a coffin, preferably an expensive one, but if my way – why not standing up? – the strain on my neck upside down is too much for them to bear. I tell them all the nutritional goodness is now in my brain and upper body. Hardly a thing of value is below my waist – they can trust me on that – so let's go deepest with the best.

Acknowledgments

I thank Yael Goldstein Love for a superb job editing this book. I thank Robert Sacks for help with the photos, Steve St. Pierre for the cover and Justin Keenan for the layout. I thank Jeffrey Epstein for supplying an early vision of how the chapters might be organized and the Ann and Gordon Getty and Enhanced Learning Foundations for their support.

About the Author

Robert Trivers is a professor of anthropology and biological sciences at Rutgers University. Winner of the Crafoord Prize, he was recognized for "his fundamental analysis of social evolution, conflict, and cooperation." Trivers lives in Somerset, New Jersey, and in Jamaica.

CPSIA information can be obtained at www.ICGtesting.com
Printed in the USA
LVOW11s2239250216

476712LV00004BA/218/P

9 781938 972126